**New Directions for
Community Colleges**

Arthur M. Cohen
EDITOR-IN-CHIEF

Richard L. Wagoner
ASSOCIATE EDITOR

Gabriel Jones
MANAGING EDITOR

Technology Management

Tod Treat
EDITOR

Number 154 • Summer 2011
Jossey-Bass
San Francisco

TECHNOLOGY MANAGEMENT
Tod Treat (ed.)
New Directions for Community Colleges, no. 154

Arthur M. Cohen, Editor-in-Chief
Richard L. Wagoner, Associate Editor
Gabriel Jones, Managing Editor

NEW DIRECTIONS FOR COMMUNITY COLLEGES (ISSN 0194-3081, electronic ISSN 1536-0733) is part of The Jossey-Bass Higher and Adult Education Series and is published quarterly by Wiley Subscription Services, Inc., A Wiley Company, at Jossey-Bass, 989 Market Street, San Francisco, CA 94103-1741. Periodicals Postage Paid at San Francisco, California, and at additional mailing offices. POSTMASTER: Send address changes to New Directions for Community Colleges, Jossey-Bass, 989 Market Street, San Francisco, CA 94103-1741.

SUBSCRIPTIONS cost $89.00 for individuals and $259.00 for institutions, agencies, and libraries in the United States. Prices subject to change.

EDITORIAL CORRESPONDENCE should be sent to the Editor-in-Chief, Arthur M. Cohen, at the Graduate School of Education and Information Studies, University of California, Box 951521, Los Angeles, CA 90095-1521. All manuscripts receive anonymous reviews by external referees.

New Directions for Community Colleges is indexed in CIJE: Current Index to Journals in Education (ERIC), Contents Pages in Education (T&F), Current Abstracts (EBSCO), Ed/Net (Simpson Communications), Education Index/Abstracts (H. W. Wilson), Educational Research Abstracts Online (T&F), ERIC Database (Education Resources Information Center), and Resources in Education (ERIC).

Microfilm copies of issues and articles are available in 16mm and 35mm, as well as microfiche in 105mm, through University Microfilms Inc., 300 North Zeeb Road, Ann Arbor, MI 48106-1346.

CONTENTS

TECHNOLOGY MANAGEMENT AND THE COMMUNITY COLLEGE: AN INTRODUCTION

Tod Treat

Technology management incorporates planning, directing, control, and coordination of technological capabilities in an organization. The appropriate development and implementation of technologies can shape and help accomplish the strategic and operational objectives of an organization (Task Force on Management of Technology, 1987). Planning what an organization will need in terms of technology, identifying hardware and software solutions, or deciding what should be purchased or built in-house requires systematic and sound management practices. In addition, technology management requires development of sound policies and leadership for effective coordination, design, and forecasting (Liao, 2005).

Organizations have very different approaches to technology management. For some institutions, the chief information officer (CIO) role focuses on infrastructure maintenance, project management, or security. For other institutions, technology management is strategic—targeting technical strategy to align and enhance other elements of the core business; developing enterprise architectures that effectively harness organizational capabilities; building analytics that enhance the organization's growth and quality; or building models that effectively source, distribute, train, and implement technological tools. Finally, as agents in a knowledge economy, some institutions have begun to integrate technology management and knowledge management, developing elaborate systems that harness knowledge through both technological and people resources.

At the community college, the institutional alignment close to industry, high level of accountability, and rapid response to local needs all contribute to a dynamic environment in which the institution's strategy related to technology management takes on critical dimensions, particularly the need to collaborate across institutional lines, such as academic services, student services, human resources, and financial services.

The purpose of this volume of *New Directions for Community Colleges* is to explore technology management from a variety of vantage points. My hope is that the volume will serve both practitioners and researchers. Community colleges are doing a great deal with both technology and knowledge management, providing rich opportunities for research. At the same time, community college leaders are seeking ways to better leverage

NEW DIRECTIONS FOR COMMUNITY COLLEGES, no. 154, Summer 2011 © 2011 Wiley Periodicals, Inc.
Published online in Wiley Online Library (wileyonlinelibrary.com) • DOI: 10.1002/cc.441

technology for institutional research, student and organizational learning, and communications.

In Chapter One, I argue that technology management ought to be considered as a strategy equal to physical, human, and fiscal management for organizations that derive value from knowledge. I also argue against purist notions separating technology and knowledge, instead suggesting a strategy for technology management that is integrated with knowledge management.

As illustrations of this integration, two chapters discuss use of technology in reaching students. In Chapter Two, M. Craig Herndon describes development of a statewide system in Virginia intended to aid the state's students in college and career planning, reducing the advising load on individual colleges, and enhancing workforce development for the entire state by aligning skills development with workplace needed. The success of Wizard is based on significant planning, using expert advice, evaluation of existing systems, social networks and key influencers, and strategic collaborations wherever possible. By contrast, in Chapter Three, Joe Offermann and Ryan Smith speak to the importance of technological systems in institutional research and accountability and the tracking of student success on an individual campus. Together, these chapters speak to the importance of integrated reporting systems.

The volume then turns to broad considerations of teaching and learning. In Chapter Four, Regina L. Garza Mitchell offers a series of practical suggestions for planning use of instructional technologies. In Chapter Five, Susanne K. Bajt explores the potential for engaging students using Web 2.0 tools. Finally, in a nod to anticipated changes in teaching and learning, Vance S. Martin discusses in Chapter 6 the potential implementation of gaming as a core andragogical strategy.

In Chapter Seven, Bob Barber reminds us that faculty members play an important role in community colleges due to their close proximity to the core business of teaching and learning, expertise in both discipline and vocation, and creativity in areas that include technology. Shared governance should extend to technology management, he argues, or risk losing those whose adoption is so critical to successful change practices related to technology.

In Chapters Eight and Nine, we turn to those whose roles are so often linked to technology management, the Chief Information Officers. A growing number of community colleges now include CIOs in the executive team, but the role itself ranges widely: Scott Armstrong, Lauren Simer, and Lee Spaniol elucidate the role while, in Chapter Nine, Jeff Bartkovich explores the funding limitations and external considerations that make the role both exciting and potentially frustrating.

The volume ends with a chapter by Thomas Ramage, a community college president with strong ties to technology management. The purpose of this chapter is twofold. First, we must return to the characteristics that make community colleges great: a forward-thinking attitude, continuous environmental monitoring, and focus on anticipating local workforce needs. Second, we must recognize that the world we educate in is changing at an accelerating rate, and we must change along with it.

My appreciation goes out to the authors for their diligence and commitment. A number of graduate students at the University of Illinois also aided in the initial review of chapters, particularly Kyeeheon Cho, Heeyoung Han, Joey Merrin, Vance Martin, and Jeff Grider. Finally, I wish to thank the editors of *New Directions for Community Colleges* for their continued commitment to bridging research and practice and for offering a venue for dialogue and professional development that advances the community college mission.

References

Liao, S. "Technology Management Methodologies and Applications: A Literature Review from 1995 to 2003." *Technovation*, 2005, 25, 381–393.

Task Force on Management of Technology. *Management of Technology: The Hidden Competitive Advantage*. National Academy Press, Washington, D.C., 1987.

TOD TREAT *is assistant professor in the Department of Education Policy, Organization, and Leadership at the University of Illinois at Urbana-Champaign.*

1

The effective integration of planning to include bricks, bytes, brains, and bandwidth (the 4Bs) represents an opportunity for community colleges to extend their capacity as knowledge-intensive organizations, coupling knowledge, technology, and learning. Integration is important to ensure that the interplay among organizations, agents within them, and technology result in enhanced global performance within the organization rather than localized improvement that creates new difficulties elsewhere. Enhanced roles for chief information officers should include people-enhancing processes, such as learning, coaching, mentoring, and team development; attention to learning architectures that include the 4Bs; and a strategic emphasis on developing organizational intelligence through transformation of data into working knowledge.

4Bs or Not 4Bs: Bricks, Bytes, Brains, and Bandwidth

Tod Treat

Introduction

One can scarcely scan a newspaper, Web site, or business, trade, or higher education journal, or even engage in casual conversation, without hearing that we have shifted to the "knowledge economy." Indeed, one can point to the popularization of a simple graphical user interface browser called Mosaic (developed at the University of Illinois) with its ability to provide easy access to the Internet as a critical moment in human history with respect to the way we communicate, shop, learn, and entertain ourselves. But if e-mail, e-commerce, and e-learning have consumed our individual way of life, they also have reoriented organizational life. Organizations today utilize technologies to manage financial processes, energy utilization, communications, transactions of all sorts, and their core business. All knowledge-intensive organizations need technology management.

NEW DIRECTIONS FOR COMMUNITY COLLEGES, no. 154, Summer 2011 © 2011 Wiley Periodicals, Inc.
Published online in Wiley Online Library (wileyonlinelibrary.com) • DOI: 10.1002/cc.442

The community college, known for its adaptability, its efforts to learn from external partnerships, and its willingness to innovate, represents a knowledge-intensive organization. The community college has been quick to adopt technologies that can accelerate its core businesses, such as learning management systems in the 1990s, and, more recently, social networking, mobile learning, and enterprise systems. Growth, in the form of new campuses, new buildings, or new learning spaces, is often accompanied by a new suite of technologies. In such situations, "structuring" can lead to profound change before areas of the institutions are well-prepared. Additionally, the hiring of new personnel can create conflict between digital immigrants and digital natives. As with other knowledge-intensive organizations, the ability of the community college to manage its resources must extend beyond physical, human, and fiscal resources to include technological resources.

Why the 4Bs Matter

When decisions related to building, people, hardware, or software are made by institutions independently, the solutions may meet local needs but may begin a process of change, of restructuring, that may lead to new problems elsewhere.

Management scholars point to knowledge workers and their interactions with technology as key drivers in organizations. Indeed, Perrow (1967, p. 195) argued that technology, which he defined as "work being done in organizations," is the "defining characteristic" of technology. Theorists such as Orlikowski (1992), Barley (1986), and others have looked at the impact of technology on structuring organizations and on culture. Technology both structures and is structured by the organizations in which it resides. And as constructs populated by individuals, organizations are mediated by the people who use technologies. Introduction of technologies for learning, communication, transactions, accountability, or productivity are as impactful on organizations as the bricks and mortar that make up the physical infrastructure or the personnel decisions that drive human resources.

Community college leaders know that the quality, motivation, and creativity of faculty and staff are key to success in efforts to help students learn and grow. We have become accustomed to the notion that our physical architecture—our "bricks"—can have a significant impact on how we perceive activity, communicate with each other, and learn. The connection between bricks and brains is something that we consider when we extend our campuses; build new laboratories to be more collaborative; introduce simulated clinical spaces, shop floors, and "situation rooms" to model workplaces more authentically; or renew our libraries to encourage interaction rather than isolation. Technology needs often are considered as well, and many institutions have computer rotation plans, servers and databases,

NEW DIRECTIONS FOR COMMUNITY COLLEGES • DOI: 10.1002/cc

Wi-Fi hot spots, and advanced systems of bandwidth distribution and security. As theorists would point out, however, greater consideration is needed of the *interactions among* our physical spaces, our virtual spaces, and our individual and organizational learning. The four Bs of bricks, bytes, brains, and bandwidth are interconnected and interrelated. They must be coupled.

Coupling Knowledge, Technology, and Learning

Institutions that organize for learning find ways to couple technology and knowledge management. Learning organizations are those that use prior experience, research, analysis, and sharing to make decisions, feeding learned practices back through the organization. As outlined by Argyris and Schon (1978), organizational learning includes both single-loop learning, fixing the immediate problem by improved efficiency or effectiveness, and double-loop learning, oriented toward understanding and mitigating the root causes of a problem. Double-loop learning challenges underlying assumptions, values, and theories in use (models and practices). Colleges that successfully link technology and knowledge into learning loops will be better able to realize competitive advantage by augmenting and extending core competencies. Learning organizations create new knowledge by design or transfer new competencies in four ways: search, learn, purchase, or collaboration. As institutions improve, their ability to take discrete new knowledge and apply it more broadly through adaptation or appropriation can lead to increased absorptive capacity, enhancing and accelerating learning.

For community colleges attuned to meeting vast community needs with limited financial resources, knowledge management often is linked to enrollment and finances. Enterprise resource systems increasingly link student academic actions to financial aid and financial aid to business offices. Such linkages are crucial to successful efficiency, but they are insufficient to drive learning. Linkages between student enrollment and success, often housed in institutional research offices, create opportunity both for reflection (i.e., what happened to these students, did they succeed, where did they go?) and prediction (i.e., identifying and intervening when risk factors suggest difficulty completing). Finally, an institution's performance and strategy are enhanced when it effectively converts data into information and information into use, or "working knowledge." An example might be the use of data to create a balanced scorecard that measures performance against benchmarked goals.

Two forms of knowledge inform practice: explicit and tacit knowledge. Explicit knowledge is knowledge that is easy to codify and transfer. Policies, statistics, standard operating procedures, and forms can all be stored and shared from even rudimentary forms of knowledge management systems. Complicated processes and explanatory feedback, such as guidance related to curriculum development and approval, also can be shared, but the system might need to provide a degree of flexibility to accommodate modifications or differences. However, the measures of performance and success, and the steps and approaches, can be expressed easily. Tools that can manage explicit knowledge include intranets, file systems, and training regarding when and how to deliver updates to documentation.

Tacit knowledge, however, is another matter entirely. Tacit knowledge represents forms of knowledge that are developed with experience within individuals and teams. Tacit knowledge is the know-how that comes with expertise (Nonaka, 1995), and its transfer is not simply a matter of documentation. Instead, tacit knowledge is developed by close interaction between expert and novice, including mentoring, coaching, just-in-time (JIT) training, and immediate feedback. Transfer of tacit knowledge can be mediated by use of Web 2.0 tools, including blogs, forums, wikis, teleconferencing, and other interactive tools.

The connections between knowledge and technology, and between tacit and explicit knowledge, can be observed through the presence of two cycles at work in institutions' attempts to leverage knowledge through technology management. The first is the "back end," organized by "knowledge engineers." The back end consists of databases and repositories intended to create, organize, formalize, distribute, and modify data in the hope of creating opportunities for that data to be transformed into information. The second is the "front end," or user interface, where information is applied, explored, analyzed, and acted on in the course of learning and unlearning. The front and back end interact as two cycles in which new knowledge generates new applications of data, in turn generating new knowledge (Wang, 2004). This iterative process is essential to a well-designed system for knowledge management and relies heavily on technology systems that are robust enough to allow storage and manipulation of data but user friendly enough to be used by stakeholders, such as student services staff, faculty, or administrators, at the point of service.

Learning Communities

Social structures are crucial to knowledge sharing and include work groups, teams, strategic and learning communities, communities of practice, and networks, differentiated by purpose, formality, type of knowledge, membership, duration, and boundaries. Each of these structures has different characteristics and thus might be expected to rely on technology for mediation in different ways (Blankenship and Ruona, 2009).

As an outgrowth of Lave and Wenger's (1991) communities of practice, virtual communities of practice (VCoP) represent the kind of fluid triage teams that can contribute to community college efficacy regardless of institutional size. Communities of practice form whenever groups or teams, organized around a unifying theme, share and learn from their experiences. But where communities of practice typically are face to face, VCoPs form using online tools, such as discussion boards in intranets, chat, or videoconferencing.

VCoPs can provide a mechanism for tacit knowledge sharing by allowing organizational members to raise and explore issues, or seek solutions, within targeted groups. Effective use of VCoPs, and with knowledge management strategies in general, cannot occur without broad participation of the members of the organization. In addition to *performance concerns*— comparing infrastructure, cost, time and effort, and training needs to ultimate improvement in service, retention, and outcomes—planning and implementation requires attention to several dimensions of the organization: *cultural norms* related to knowledge sharing and use of technology, *utilization concerns* related to usefulness and ease of use, and *collaborative concerns* regarding member trust, willingness to share, accountability, and reciprocity (Ardichvili and Yoon, 2009).

Creation of VCoPs clearly requires more than a technical solution. Social solutions, such as personal benefits, community building, and incentives, must be incorporated while removing barriers to use such as fear, lack of technical skill or understanding of technology tools, or power differentials. Likewise, enabling activities, such as a supportive corporate culture, useful tool development, and leadership, contribute to development of open exchange, expertise development, and creation of narratives that contribute to a sense of common purpose and relationship (Ardichvili, 2008).

Creating Learning Architectures

For community colleges, learning architectures that cull information from student or employee activity often are underdeveloped or ignored entirely. In particular, the use of learning architectures to inform and advance practice, if they exist, may be disconnected from real-time activity such as registration, research, instruction, or student support. Divisions and departments may develop homegrown tools to facilitate local needs, often using "screen scrapes" from a mainframe instead of direct manipulation of data. These tools meet local needs but undermine institutional needs to ensure database integrity and common results for use in interpretation. At the same time, the decision to centralize technology management processes can lead to complicated, if sometimes combative, debates among institutional researchers, instructional technology staff, faculty, and others, all of whom have specific ideas about system use and, since form follows function, structure. Thus, relationship building and process mapping may play roles that are more important than specific technology questions.

Just as formal learning is facilitated by sound instructional design, so, too, is organizational learning. Van Merrienboer, Clark, and de Croock (2002) describe instructional design for complex skills development (4C-ID) that can be applied to learning systems in organizations. The application of the 4C-ID model stems from the recognition that complex skills demonstrated *in situ* represent activity that we all undertake on a daily basis at work. The 4C-ID model aims to overcome three deficits common in both formal and informal learning: (1) lack of integration of knowledge and skills, (2) lack of distinction between JIT instruction and supportive information, and (3) use of both part-task and whole-task practice. Four elements are part of the design: (1) inductive learning tasks focus on authentic whole-task practice; (2) supportive information, which may include documentation, schematics, policies, data and analysis examples, and so on; (3) JIT information, which is targeted and fades as learners develop expertise; and (4) part-task practice. These four elements may be equally valuable in a formal system devoted to classroom learning or in an informal system devoted to organizational learning. Additionally, a well-designed system will have standards, metadata, and packaging that allow for seamless use, updating, and reuse (Horton, 2006). In such a system, producers provide the inputs needed to populate the system, but the front-end presentation to end-users is customized according to need.

Curricular analogies exist between formal course-based learning, which increasingly utilizes learning management systems, and organizational learning, which utilizes knowledge management systems. Both make efforts to codify what is being learned, collect data, and provide structures for data management. Both learning management and knowledge management systems can utilize activities and transformation tools. Both contain repositories that house files and resources that can be organized and stored. Both contain presentation and analytic tools facilitated by metadata. Thus, the application of proven instructional design principles, such as those just outlined, improves the functioning, use, and benefit of technology-based organizational systems.

Naismith and others (2004) suggest that technology plans consider technologies along two continua: level of use and portability. Devices that are static and individual, such as clickers or computer labs, present institutions with an ability to use diagnostic or placement software, tutorials, or classroom response pedagogies. Static but collaborative devices, such as videoconferencing or capture software on interactive whiteboards, stretch the ability of faculty to reach students in time and space. Portable collaborative devices such as kiosks facilitate experiential learning *in situ*. But mobile, individual learning utilizing laptops, tablet computing, smart phones, or even at-home gaming systems present opportunities for as-yet-unrealized personalized learning that truly can take place anywhere and might, perhaps, be best facilitated by modeling student interaction with technology in noninstructional spaces, such as retail, transportation, environmental, or cultural spaces. How will learners receive information? Horton (2006) suggests multiple avenues of content delivery, including formal presentations, handouts, and notes available in pdf or other formats, formal reports, virtual learning spaces with discussion boards, and mobile learning distribution such as podcasts or social media.

NEW DIRECTIONS FOR COMMUNITY COLLEGES • DOI: 10.1002/cc

Organizational Intelligence

Organizational intelligence is another aspect of technology management that provides an institution with enhanced capabilities. Davenport and Harris (2009) describe organizational intelligence as having mechanisms that can take businesses processes, generate data from them, "extract, transform, and load" elements into a data warehouse, and, in a regular and systematic way, use the data for predictive analysis, reporting, and performance assessment. Intelligence results not from having these mechanisms but from using them to advance from reports to benchmarks, diagnoses, forecasting, predictive modeling, and scenario planning that ultimately lead to optimization of core business processes. For the community college, that might mean being able to track a student from point of entry to point of exit and, using past data, predict what new entering students might need as they initiate contact with the institution. Or business intelligence might mean tracking an individual student's successes and challenges in the curriculum and generating individualized learning plans intended to stimulate successful completion. Faculty performance might be assessed based on increasingly attenuated points of emphasis in areas such as retention, persistence, or student success in subsequent courses or upon entering the work world. Finally, analytics might provide guidance in determining which community partnerships are providing the institution with opportunities and which ones need more careful attention. To work properly, systems must have architectures that store data, processes to transform that data, tools to analyze that data, and end-user reports that present the data in ways that communicate effectively, such as dashboards, graphs, and tables.

Analytics have long powered commercial enterprises like Amazon, Netflix, Capital One, or Google. In fact, Davenport and Harris (2009) highlight thirty-two well-known firms from a variety of sectors that compete on analytics. But how useful are analytics for education? No doubt, sophisticated analytic models exist for identifying and customizing outreach to potential students who have queried a college Web site. But the best example of analytics at a community college is from Rio Salado College. Located in Tempe, Arizona, Rio Salado is part of the Maricopa Community College District. With nearly forty thousand distance education students, Rio Salado operates on a novel model using individualized learning plans, a home-grown learning management system, accelerated programs, and new course starts nearly every week of the year. Rio Salado is serving students across the globe and competes to ensure student success and satisfaction and to retain existing students and attract new ones. Rio Salado is using analytics to predict at-risk behavior using activity factors such as log-ins and site engagement. Based on the institution's predictive models, Rio Salado is able to predict student risk based on reduced engagement and is developing strategies for intervention, including student risk dashboards for faculty (Smith, 2010).

Putting the Information in Chief Information Officer

The role of a chief information officer (CIO), whether an executive or a faculty member on release, ranges from financial and technical issues, such as planning for and replacing office and laboratory computers, to strategic and visionary matters, such as building solutions and infrastructure to serve community partners and students. CIOs have to worry about change, data, project management, hardware and software, systems and processes, security and redundancy, users, and forecasting. The role of the CIO and of governance in general is addressed elsewhere in this volume, but the title itself is worth some consideration. What do we mean by "information," and how does it differ from the reams of data regularly generated on college campuses?

Various authors, most notably Davenport and Prusak (1998), have discussed the differences by among the terms "data," "information," "knowledge," and "working knowledge" (or knowledge in use). "Data" are unfiltered bits associated with an occurrence. We collect data continuously from our perceptions or from our systems. Due to recognition of the need to be accountable to the public, community colleges have become quite adept at collecting data. Alone, however, data have little value. "Data-driven decision making" is rather difficult without the transformation of data into information. Davenport and Prusak speak of five methods of transformation that add value to data: (1) contextualization, (2) categorization, (3) calculation, (4) correction, and (5) condensation. Taking all those bits and using them to paint a picture of an occurrence is much more valuable than merely collecting the bits themselves: They must be transformed. Even then, information alone does not lead toward understanding. Information must be combined with experience, analyzed for patterns, compared and connected, considered and discussed. Insights based on information lead to knowledge. And knowledge applied to problems is working knowledge.

Effective transformation of data to working knowledge takes energy and a continual focus on problems that need to be solved. Technology alone cannot enhance transformation of data to information to knowledge. A narrow CIO role, focusing on hardware, network, and software acquisition and support, can serve institutional needs related to faculty and student access, but it provides limited value related to enhanced processes or strategic value. People-enhancing processes, such as learning, coaching, mentoring, and team development, are equally important and might be included as part of the activities an effective CIO can be expected to perform.

Recommendations for Community Colleges

The complexity of human resources, learning space design, technology management, and organizational advancement is difficult enough to address independently of one another. Efforts to integrate the 4Bs begin

NEW DIRECTIONS FOR COMMUNITY COLLEGES • DOI: 10.1002/cc

with planning and leadership and suggest that these plans must be both intentional—to integrate successfully—and dynamic—to adapt to changes in technology and staff.

As a first step, community colleges should create an integrated campus master plan that includes all four Bs. Master plans related to physical infrastructure outline anticipated new construction on a campus based on aspirational goals. The level of detail and composition of these plans vary but generally reflect a good deal of input from various stakeholders and suggest the direction a college wishes to go. A 4B master plan would incorporate additional elements explicitly related to human capital and technology needs, in additional to physical needs.

Additionally, colleges should consider if and how current systems interact. Many institutions have evolved systems that are only marginally connected to one another. Real-time integration between online instructional delivery and institutional systems requires care and foresight. Process mapping at institutional and divisional levels provides opportunity to improve systems integration and individual processes.

At a general level, classroom design is not based on evolving pedagogical needs but on cost-per-square-foot calculations. "Smart classrooms" often reflect an increasingly incorrect assumption about how learning happens and situate technology so that it is at the front of the room. A learning system designed around the needs and preferences of students might suggest something very different; for example, an open mobile learning-capable floor plan will architecturally suggest a different approach to learning.

Organizational systems are no different. A blueprint of development of new programs, new spaces, new personnel, and new initiatives must include *explicit* consideration of how structures, personnel, and technology will interact. A learning organization, attuned to transformation of data to information and of information to knowledge, will find ways to use technology. Designing learning systems first and then building the physical and technological infrastructure around them can lead to enhanced organizational learning.

Colleges should support an executive-level position that coordinates technology management across academic, fiscal, student, and other services. At community colleges, the executive portfolio typically contains vice presidents of academic services, business services, students services, and, perhaps, institutional advancement. Although each of these positions is focused a critical aspect of community college operations, technology management underpins them all. Each of these positions, and its groups, represents a specialty that relies on the infrastructure and products of technology but is not necessarily focused on it. A CIO position, like a critical care coordinator in a surgical unit, ensures that system designs do not contraindicate one another. The CIO also forecasts emerging technologies, obsolescence and replacement schedules, and platform changes to manage continuous data collection and service. And, when a community college has optimized its knowledge and technology management, the CIO is as engaged in development of people as in acquisition of technology tools. Indeed, successful knowledge and technology management can occur only when technology toolbox use is matched to the needs and abilities of employees within the specific institution.

Finally, dynamic change exists in both the technology and its end users, requiring that colleges consider end users today as well as tomorrow. As Generation X employees and Millennials begin predominating in institutions as both employees and students, technology capabilities, needs, and expectations will shift from individual productivity software on desktops to increasingly mobile and interactive apps. Few colleges are delivering mobile learning to students effectively. Fewer still are considering the impact of a new wave of employee expectations regarding how time, space, and inter-activity impact productivity. Incorporating younger, technology-savvy employees and students in the technology-planning process, focusing on principles rather than on specific platforms or software, will aid in transitioning institutions to providing service and productivity needs to a wide array of users.

Bricks, Bytes, Brains, and Bandwidth

The premise of this chapter is straightforward, but its implementation is complex: Community colleges intent on fully harnessing their capabilities must plan for all four Bs: bricks, bytes, brains, and bandwidth. The physical infrastructure, technology resources, human capital, and network capabilities all must be managed in an integrated fashion toward realization of a learning organization. However, size, scope, and resources matter, and the challenges for a small rural college or a large multi-college district to create integrated systems will no doubt vary. Creation of a learning-oriented culture will lead to better results as technologies are adopted, particularly if adoption is part of an inclusive 4B planning process. Knowledge management and technology management are coupled as part of effective organizational learning and can be integrated according to proven instructional design principles to produce effective organizational learning. When considered together the 4Bs can contribute to both virtual communities of practice (VCoP) across the institution and enhanced organizational intelligence: the systematic collection, transformation, and, most important, use of information in regular and systematic ways to improve college performance in service to our students and our communities.

References

Ardichvili, A. "Learning and Knowledge Sharing in Virtual Communities of Practice: Motivators, Barriers, and Enablers." *Advances in Developing Human Resources*, 2008, *10*(4), 541–554.

Ardichvili, A., and Yoon, S. W. "Designing integrative knowledge management systems: considerations and practical applications." *Advances in Developing Human Resources*, 2009, *11*(3), 307–319.

Argyris, C. and Schon, D. A. *Organizational Learning: A Theory of Action Perspective.* Reading, Mass.: Addison-Wesley, 1978.

Barley, S. R. "Technology as an Occasion for Structuring: Evidence from Observations of CT Scanners and the Social Order of Radiology Departments." *Administrative Science Quarterly*, 1986, *31*(1), 78–108.

Blankenship, S. S., and Ruona, W. E. "Exploring Knowledge Sharing in Social Structures: Potential Contributions to an Overall Knowledge Management Strategy." *Advances in Developing Human Resources*, 2009, *11*(3), 290–306.

Davenport, T. H., and Harris, J. G. *Competing on Analytics.* Cambridge, Mass.: Harvard Business School Press, 2007.

Davenport, T. H., and Prusak, L. *Working Knowledge: How Organizations Manage What They Know.* Cambridge, Mass.: Harvard University Press, 1998.

Horton, W. K. *E-learning by design.* San Francisco: Pfeiffer, 2006.

Lave, J., and Wenger, E. *Situated Learning: Legitimate Peripheral Participation.* New York: Cambridge University Press, 1991.

Naismith, L., and others. "Literature Review in Mobile Technologies and Learning," Report 11. NESTA Futurelab Series. Bristol, U.K., 2004.

Nonaka, I. A Dynamic Theory of Organizational Knowledge Creation. *Organization Science,* 1995, *5*(1), 14–37.

Orlikowski, W. J. "The Duality of Technology: Rethinking the Concept of Technology in Organizations." *Organization* Science, 1992, *3*(3), 398–427.

Perrow, C. "A Framework for the Analysis of Organizations." *American Sociological Review*, 1967, *32*(2), 194–208.

Smith, V. "Action Analytics to Increase Online Student Engagement and Success." Presentation at CQIN Summer Institute. Fort Collins, Colo., August 2, 2010.

Van Merrienboer, J. J. G.; Clark, R. E.; and de Croock, M. B. M. "Blueprints for Complex Learning: The 4C/ID Model." *Educational Technology Research and Development,* 2002, *50*(2), 39–64.

Wang, S., and Ariguzo, G. "Knowledge Management through the Development of Information Schema." *Information and Management*, 2003, *41*, 445–456.

TOD TREAT is assistant professor in the Department of Education Policy, Organization, and Leadership at the University of Illinois at Urbana-Champaign.

NEW DIRECTIONS FOR COMMUNITY COLLEGES • DOI: 10.1002/cc

2

The use of Web technologies to connect with and disperse information to prospective and current students can be effective for students as well as efficient for colleges. Early results of the use of such technologies in a statewide system point to high rates of satisfaction among students when information is delivered, provide clues on how various aspects of social media may be tapped to connect with existing and potential students, and offer a road map for effectively serving more students with fewer resources. The chapter concludes with a discussion of future applications for Web-based technologies in multiplying the efforts of good academic counseling techniques to better serve and retain students.

Leveraging Web Technologies in Student Support Self-Services

M. Craig Herndon

In 2006, Glenn DuBois, chancellor of the Virginia Community College System, was making arrangements for a trip to Ireland and was struck by how travel planning had shifted from an activity that once required a travel agent to one that now relied on self-service, Web-based technologies. He immediately began to ponder if such self-service technologies could help students in planning for careers. With this vision, he sought and received federal funding to support the development of the Virginia Education Wizard—a one-stop career and college planning tool that provides self-service to current and potential students to help them make informed decisions, thereby alleviating some of the personnel-intensive student services burdens placed on colleges and facilitating economic efficiency by guiding citizens to high-pay, high-demand occupations and the education and financial resources needed to obtain them.

This chapter describes the development and use of a specific self-service Web technology to connect with and disperse information to

NEW DIRECTIONS FOR COMMUNITY COLLEGES, no. 154, Summer 2011 © 2011 Wiley Periodicals, Inc.
Published online in Wiley Online Library (wileyonlinelibrary.com) • DOI: 10.1002/cc.443

prospective and current students in ways that are familiar to and effective for students as well as efficient for the colleges and economically beneficial for communities.

Context

Community colleges are facing record enrollment growths and budget shortfalls (Borden, 2008; Bushong, 2009; Carr, 2009) at a time when postsecondary-education is becoming increasingly more important to obtaining employment in the new economy (Carnevale, Smith, and Stroh, 2010). As is well documented in both theory and practice, community college enrollments tend to rise, if not surge, when the economy contracts (Betts and McFarland, 1995). A multidecade decline in public funding for higher education in concert with a sharp economic contraction produces particular hardship for community colleges, given their reliance on state and local funding for the greatest share of their nontuition and fee revenue (Cohen and Brawer, 2008; Gumport and Pusser, 1997). This combination of growing enrollment and that funding reduction serves as an impetus for many colleges to innovate.

At the same time colleges are facing significant challenges to meet the growing demand for services and to do so with fewer resources, consumers are experiencing greater access to self-service technologies in other realms (Bitner, Ostrom, and Meuter, 2002; Castor, Atkinson, and Ezell, 2010). The term "self-service technology" (SST) refers to any technology that allows customers to produce services without direct involvement of human resources (Zeithaml, Bitner, and Gremler, 2009). It can include a wide range of services from airport kiosks that permit travelers to check in to flights, to automatic bank teller machines, to the various purchasing and services available via the Internet. SSTs are adopted to provide greater convenience to consumers and greater efficiency to the providing organization.

Among consumers of community college education, and particularly among Millennials, there is a growing use of technology to engage with their environment (Center for Community College Student Engagement, 2009). While community colleges are on par or surpass other public institutions of higher education when it comes to delivering their primary goal—that is, education—via the Web (Allen and Seaman, 2007), and while a number of public and private institutions use SSTs for financial and auxiliary services such as tuition payment, meal plan modification, parking services, and access to library materials, institutions of higher education offer relatively few student support self-services via SSTs.

Colleges interested in developing and implementing student SSTs may benefit from lessons learned via the development, implementation, and early analysis of a new tool produced by the Virginia Community College System to support student decision making in planning for careers and college. This chapter describes the development, implementation, and early analysis of one such SST, the Virginia Education Wizard. The essential guideposts in a road map for producing such technology are then discussed.

Developing a Career and College Planning Tool

The Virginia Community College System (VCCS) serves more than 370,000 people annually through credit instruction and noncredit workforce development training at twenty-three colleges on forty campuses. The development of a student support SST by the VCCS began with an assessment of student need for student services and an assessment of the resources already in place to support student services. The process for assessing student need began by seeking to identify the most pressing questions that current and potential students faced in planning for and navigating through postsecondary education and on their way to four-year institutions and careers. In addition, and instructed by literature, the student assessment sought to identify the means by which students most preferred to obtain answers to their most pressing questions (Center for Community College Student Engagement, 2009). In conducting this assessment, it was assumed that a richer set of data would come from querying not only students but also those who frequently provide support services to them. A statewide survey of college faculty and student services staff as well as a survey of students at two community colleges in Virginia was administered.

Analyzing the Need. The surveys illuminated three major themes as well as some additional information that would help shape the development of student support SST. First, students reported that they most valued and had the least access to information on paying for college and that choosing a career and choosing a major were secondary to that concern. Second, those who serve students indicated that students were in most need of information pertaining to selecting potential occupations and determining the appropriate program of study leading to their desired occupations. Third, the surveys administered to students, of varying ages, also indicated that students were frequently engaged in self-advising with regard to career and college planning, that they perceived that they had limited or disparate tools at their disposal to do so, and that they had interest in and frequently preferred to receive student support information via interactive, Web-based technology.

Following the survey of students and those who serve them, an internal inventory was developed to identify a set of tools and information that were used by students and those who serve them, as well as an evaluation to determine what, if any, resources used by community college students were successful in guiding student decision making, and the relative effectiveness of such tools in meeting their intended aim. The resources' effectiveness was then measured by the degree to which the resources were utilized, comprehensive, current, and accessible. By juxtaposing the student needs identified by the survey with the inventory and evaluation of resources, the needs-gap analysis helped to reveal that critical sources of information and tools to help students make informed decisions were often out-of-date, incomplete, missing, or in a format that was incompatible with students' preference for receiving information via Web-based sources. The VCCS next undertook an external environmental scan to identify potential technology solutions. No comprehensive technology solution sets existed to meet the scope of the needs identified by students, faculty, and staff.

Developing a Structure. With the identification of needs and resources and an understanding that no single tool existed to meet the comprehensive needs identified, an advisory committee—comprised of leaders from community colleges and the statewide system office—constructed a framework for the development of a new and comprehensive student support SST. Informed by the analysis of needs and resources, the strategic plan of the VCCS in place at the time the project was initiated, and literature on creating SSTs, guiding principles were established. The student support SST would seek to address those needs expressed by students, faculty, and staff and would aim to do so in an easy-to-use, sustainable format that delivered high-quality information to users (Bitner and others, 2002; Shu-Hsun and Ying-Yin, 2008). The information in the student support SST would guide students and potential students in career and college decision-making, thereby contributing to the development of a workforce whose skills are better aligned with the needs of the economy while reducing the burden on college staff to provide information that could be delivered more efficiently by technology (Castor and others, 2010; VCCS, 2003). Moreover, the project advisory committee recommended that the tool, like any SST, should provide information and resources for current and potential students on topics and at levels of depth that could be sufficiently addressed through self-service, avoiding sophisticated levels of response and processing that are required of human resources.

To carry out its vision, the project advisory committee identified five major areas for which the tool should deliver student support SST: (1) career planning, (2) academic planning in the form of selecting a major or program, (3) paying for college, (4) planning for community college admission, and (5) college transfer planning. The committee then organized five work groups, comprised of experts in the respective content areas from around the state, to identify the best possible information and resources needed by students to make informed decisions and to act as safeguards in advancing content that was suitable for self-service.

Charges to the five work groups conveyed the advisory committee's commitment to an easy-to-use, sustainable tool that delivered high-quality information. As one work group member said, "The trick is to provide sophisticated information that is individually tailored to the unique user, and to do so in a way that even the least tech-savvy among us can access and make sense of it."

Building and Editing. After the work groups helped to identify the functions that the student support SST should perform and the information that it should provide for each functional area for the tools, all groups participated in a process of reviewing and editing the project's various tools while the tools were under development. Prototypes were created and shared with the work groups for comment, and amendments were made as the theoretical became tangible. In addition, various components of the student support SST were shared with student groups in an effort to gain feedback. The iterative process of reviewing, editing, and improving the component tools was carried out for a period of months before the system of tools that comprise the student SST was shared with small student groups for testing. The result of collecting feedback from the work groups and students was the incremental improvement of each component of the student support SST over several months. The process was concluded naturally when the feedback from work groups and students began to dwindle and consensus began to emerge around readiness for releasing the components to a larger audience for testing.

Following the conclusion of testing with work groups and small groups of students, a large-scale test of the student support SST was conducted on the integrated and fully-functional career- and college-planning tool, which was by this time called the Virginia Education Wizard. The result of the testing process identified very high levels of satisfaction with usability and content for individual tools, and the entire site was deemed ready for implementation.

Implementation

In planning to introduce and sustain the growth of this new technology, the VCCS chose to use a blend of social media, earned media, and policy initiatives. The use of social media provided a three-part benefit in that it afforded opportunities not only to introduce the Wizard to users but to keep them apprised of new developments to the site and to receive feedback from users that ultimately would improve the utility of the student support SST.

Social Media. Given that the Wizard's development was inspired by Web technologies, the Wizard itself is entirely Web-based, and that many of its potential users, particularly those aged fourteen to twenty-five, are engaged with social media outlets (Center for Community College Student Engagement, 2009), it seemed appropriate to focus on the use of social media and Web-based advertising as part of a combination of implementation strategies. Prior to launching the Wizard, a presence was created for the Web site and its personal guide and avatar, "Ginny," on a variety of social media platforms including, Facebook, Twitter, MySpace, LinkedIn,

Flickr, and YouTube. Using these platforms, members of the various social media communities were introduced to the Wizard in order to generate interest prior to the site's launch. Thought leaders, or influencers, in education and technology were targeted with information about the Wizard prior to and just following its launch. As a result, many chose to feature, via tweets or updates, the Wizard Web site, thereby seeding the social media outlets with interest in and praise for the site as it launched.

Policy Efforts. In addition to using social media, key influencers, and earned media to launch and sustain growth of the site, efforts were undertaken to institutionalize the Wizard through policy initiatives. Through a formal collaboration between the VCCS and the state's governing agency for public education, the coordinating agency for all higher education, a private loan guarantor, and the state's college savings plan corporation, the Wizard was designated as the statewide portal for career and college planning. This designation carried special weight in light of a 2009 action by Virginia's Board of Education that required all students, starting in seventh grade, to form personal career and college plans. Through the collaboration, the Wizard is to become the venue for forming and maintaining those plans in school districts across the state. In support of this collaboration and the implementation of academic and career plans, training sessions were developed and delivered statewide to more than twelve hundred school counselors.

Policy efforts and complementary training efforts also were undertaken to institutionalize the Wizard's use among those who work directly with students in the role of career coaches. Career coaches work in high schools to help students define their career aspirations and to recognize community college and other postsecondary programs, including apprenticeships and workforce training, that can help students achieve their educational and financial goals. Approximately 120 career coaches serve in 165 high schools across Virginia and provide individual and small-group services to 88,000 students annually. In an academic year, they assist more than 28,000 students with developing career plans and more than 30,000 students with career assessments. Statewide, career coaches are directed to use the Wizard in delivering career-planning information and career assessments and, with training provided by the VCCS, provide training to their local communities on the use of the Wizard.

In an effort to institutionalize the Wizard's use among community college students, a statewide task force charged with reviewing and making recommendations for the improvement of all student success courses delivered by Virginia's community colleges recommended that the Wizard be used as an integral component of such courses, thereby reinforcing the Wizard's use in community colleges and among new students, who constitute the largest portion of enrollment in such courses. Policy initiatives aimed at secondary and community college students, as well as those who serve them, intend to fuel usage of the Wizard and ultimately improve the amount of high-quality career and college-planning information reaching Virginians.

NEW DIRECTIONS FOR COMMUNITY COLLEGES • DOI: 10.1002/cc

Early Analysis of Use

In developing the Wizard, the VCCS sought to (1) improve information on career and college planning available to prospective and current students, thereby permitting them to navigate the process more easily and efficiently, to (2) reduce the burden on college advising and school counseling personnel in the delivery of routine information that can more effectively and reliably be delivered by technology, thereby permitting them to focus on more sophisticated needs, and (3) contribute to the production of a workforce whose skills are better aligned with the needs of the economy. An early analysis of the Wizard's use was undertaken sixteen months after the Wizard was released to the public, not to determine if it had achieved the overarching aims of the project as its relatively short lifespan would prohibit such goals from being fully realized, but to gauge indicators of how the tool was being used so that interventions could be taken where appropriate and the project could be steered toward its long term goals if needed. These early indictors included metrics on the use of financial aid information, career and college planning information, transfer information, and satisfaction with the site's content and functionality.

The analysis of Wizard usage was conducted using data collected by and stored in the site's database, records of Wizard users matched against the VCCS student files, and data derived from an external Web analytics tool that generates reports and statistics about visitors to the Wizard Web site. The analysis of satisfaction was produced using survey data derived primarily from student users but with additional surveys from those who serve students. The results, where possible at the early stage of implementation, identify the site's effectiveness in meeting its objectives and correlations between student usage and success.

Early Analysis of Effectiveness. Analyses were performed to provide an initial gauge of the site's effectiveness in meeting a set of objectives. Although the site existed for just sixteen months at the time it was analyzed, early data were available (but not considered stable enough to be more than descriptive or correlative) on three key objectives of the site.

First, the site was intended to provide information to help students answer critical questions about financial aid. Early indicators of usage identified that some 7,500 users of the site had created personalized financial aid award estimates, and that there had been a total of 23,000 pages viewed to compare the cost of colleges and universities in Virginia, almost 5,000 views of a video tutorial on completing federal financial aid forms, and almost 40,000 page views of a scholarship search tool. An examination of the receipt of financial aid among community college students revealed that 29 percent of those who had created accounts in the Wizard had received aid as compared to 26 percent of those who had not created accounts in the Wizard.

Second, the site was intended to provide information to help students plan for careers and college, thereby improving student success in college.

Early indicators show that of the nearly 4.2 million total pages viewed on the Wizard Web site, more than 1.5 million were of the career planning section. Within that section, users of the Wizard tool took more than 100,000 career assessments and saved more than 230,000 careers in their personal profiles. In planning for college, users of the site had saved some 20,000 college majors and programs to their personal profiles. Collectively, these figures identified broad use of the Wizard's career- and college-planning tools. In looking exclusively at community college students, an examination of the first-term grade point average (GPA) among Wizard users and nonusers identified that 46 percent of users earned a GPA of 3.0 or greater while only 38 percent of nonusers earned a GPA of 3.0 or greater. The percentage of users and nonusers with a first-term GPA of 2.0 to 2.99 was nearly identical, and the percentage of Wizard users with GPAs of less than a 2.0 was 24 percent as compared to 31 percent among nonusers. These results are all the more intriguing given that 41 percent of the Wizard users enrolled in developmental education and, by definition, were less prepared for college-level work, while just over a quarter of nonusers were enrolled in developmental education.

Third, the Wizard was intended to assist students in making good decisions about transfer, including selecting appropriate transfer agreements and completing associate degrees before transferring to four-year institutions. Users of the Wizard examined tens of thousands of transfer agreements available in the site's database and saved more than 7,000 transfer agreements to their profiles. Users of the Wizard also created more than 8,500 user-specific plans for transferring from a community college to a university. These plans provided step-by-step and personalized guidance in transfer and were delivered via e-mail to the students each semester, as a reminder list of things to accomplish in preparing for transfer. The Wizard's transfer planning tool includes information that underscores the financial value and credit recognition efficiency that stems from completing the associate's degree. Further analysis found that among students who created a transfer plan, 74 percent indicated that they planned to complete their associate's degree before transferring.

Actionable Items. Following the analysis, a set of actionable items was developed to advance the goals of the project. Three examples of such actionable items include those pertaining to targeting specific school divisions for Wizard use, implementing paid advertising on search engines and social media sites, and revamping the main page of the site to deemphasize account creation. As part of the analysis, users younger than eighteen years were segregated by their zip code and by the time of day that they accessed the site. A picture of how the site was being used during traditional school hours and within Virginia's school divisions emerged. This picture permits, among other things, the VCCS to reinforce the site's use in counties and cities with high utilization while seeking to improve utilization in localities with low utilization. By examining the means by which the site was being accessed and considering the correlations between increases in visits and the use of advertising, plans were enacted to advertise the Wizard on additional Web sites. Advertising was established with Google such that the entry of specific search terms from computers with Virginia IP addresses resulted in sponsored links to the Wizard. Paid advertisements were also placed on Facebook to attract additional visits to the Wizard Web site.

Early analyses of use also helped to identify a potential threat to the site's exploration by visitors drawn in by social and earned media. In the early stages of the Wizard's release, a review of data from the Web analytics tool identified a 41 percent bounce rate from the main page of the site, meaning that of all visitors to enter the site via the main page, 41 percent left without exploring any other content (Gabe, 2007). Upon reviewing the content and design of the main page and in consultation with the literature and site users, a decision was made to remove prominent buttons to sign in to the Wizard and create an account. Research suggested that by removing these prominent links, users would not assume that the site required an account, thereby encouraging usage (Spool, 2009). A focus group comprised of new site users confirmed that the removal of these links would encourage users to continue exploring the site. The site was then modified to remove these prominent buttons in favor of small links at the top of the page to log in and create an account. Reminders to log in or create an account when the user arrived at content that required an account were inserted. The result of this modification was a reduction in the bounce rate from the main page to 31 percent.

Future Analyses. The same analysis that produced descriptive site usage statistics, demographic information about users, and a set of actionable items to improve the site's function and utilization also yielded information that will require the collection of additional time-series data in order to draw more definitive conclusions. For example, the early look at the data identified correlations between Wizard use and academic success in the first semester of college. Larger data sets and the ability to track student usage of the Wizard over multiple semesters will paint a more detailed picture of this initial correlation. Moreover, future examinations will focus on evaluating the Wizard's contributions to improving the efficiency in the delivery of student services and in facilitating the development of a workforce whose skills are better aligned with the needs of the economy. For example, data derived from the Wizard's own database can help to identify specific occupations of high demand and high pay for which there is an absence of interest among citizens or an absence of education and training to prepare them.

Discussion

Despite the relatively short length of time that the Wizard has provided services to students and those who serve them, indicators identify early signs of success in serving more students with fewer resources. Evidence indicates that approximately one-third of Wizard account holders are community college students. Among this population, services that typically would require human interaction in the form of assessments delivered, questions answered, and counseling provided is now provided by a student support SST. The personnel who would have delivered services and answered questions now have additional time to address higher-level needs among the students they serve. For example, a financial aid counselor who responded to the survey of satisfaction reported that the Wizard freed up time that was once spent helping local high school students in creating personal financial aid award estimates and responding to questions from parents on completing federal financial aid forms and allowed her to reallocate that time to processing financial aid forms and granting financial aid. Comparable examples exist in the delivery of transfer information, career planning, scholarship application, and college major exploration. A road map, consisting of critical lessons drawn from the development and implementation of the Wizard, is described next.

Road Map. The development and implementation of the Wizard provides a road map that may be used by other states and colleges interested in deploying similar technology in the interest of serving more students in times of scarce resources. Although the development of any tool must consider the environment in which it will be used, a few indications imply that the Wizard may be useful in a variety of conditions.

First, the Wizard demonstrates that knowing the needs of students is critical in determining how to best serve them. At the same time, students' perception of their own needs may be incomplete. Therefore, the guidance of those faculty and staff who serve students directly is essential to providing information to assist students not just in answering their questions but also in answering the questions that professionals identify that students should ask. Students surveyed prior to the development of the Wizard indicated that paying for college was of primary concern, but their use of the Wizard has helped to identify the premium that students have placed on career planning, an area that faculty and staff deemed of much greater importance when they identified needs. With the input of students and those who serve them, the Wizard was built to deliver information on a wide range of student support topics and was not restricted to answering those questions that students deemed most important.

Second, the value of experts in developing content cannot be overstated. Web-based tools provide the unique opportunity to replicate, disperse, and keep current the good guidance of dozens of geographically dispersed experts. Engaging experts in the process helps to ensure that only sustainable information of the highest quality is selected for inclusion in the Wizard, thereby enhancing the availability of good information and reducing the threat of promulgating bad information. The contributions of experts in developing the Wizard resulted in the dissemination of information that once resided in the heads of just a few people on any college campus. That information is now readily accessible at all hours and is updated as new information is created.

Third, the evaluation of existing technical resources and tools is critical to avoiding the unnecessary duplication of resources. In building the Wizard, a limited number of tools were identified as strong resources that should be integrated with new tool sets in forming a student support SST. This strategy not only helped to avoid the needless cost of building new resources but also strengthened the value of existing resources by marrying them to a broad set of interrelated tools. For example, by tapping into an existing statewide database of the majors and programs offered by Virginia's community colleges, redundancies in information collection and maintenance were avoided. By adding new data pertaining to intended career outcomes of each major or program and presenting both in the context of a user's career assessment results, the existing information was enhanced and made more useful to consumers.

Fourth, the identification and utilization of existing social networks and key influencers for the purpose of introducing and role-modeling the use of career- and college-planning tools is essential if the tools are to be used to reach the broadest possible audience. Career coaches, who work in high schools to help students define their career aspirations and the education need to obtain them, served as Pied Pipers to high school students, faculty, and counselors. Key influencers played a similar role in publicizing the tool in social media. Social media also provided a means for users to tell their social networks about the Wizard, thereby amplifying the use of the tool.

Fifth, strategic collaborations and efforts to institutionalize the use of the Wizard through policy have and are expected to continue to expand and sustain its development and use. By collaborating with other public and private entities that aim to provide support to citizens in planning for careers and college, duplications of effort and resources are minimized. In place of many overlapping tools, a unified tool with broad political, financial, and public support can be created. By embedding the use of the Wizard in both secondary curriculum and the curriculum of community colleges, it is expected that a greater proportion of students will develop and execute academic and career plans.

Sixth, ongoing analysis and evaluation provide opportunities not only to better understand how the technology itself is being used and by whom, and to improve the delivery of information, but also to provide opportunities to better understand the needs of students and the community at large. Early analyses point to broad use of the Wizard's career- and college-planning tools and correlations between use and student success. More analysis will be essential to understanding the impact of the tool. Additional analyses also may allow Virginia's community colleges to identify high-demand and high-pay occupations for which there is an absence of interest among citizens or an absence of education and training to prepare them, and then take deliberate action to fill the workforce gap by directing citizens to those occupations or developing education and training programs.

It is expected that the development of SSTs will remain rapid in the coming years (Castor et al, 2010). The development, implementation, and early analysis of the Virginia Education Wizard offer lessons for other states and colleges interested in developing SSTs to meet growing enrollments in the face of reduced budgets. Such SSTs may provide high-quality information that enhances student success and feeds a high-quality workforce, all while sparing personnel costs. Future studies should seek to examine the long-term impact of SSTs on these perceived outcomes.

References

Allen, I. E., and Seaman, J. *Online Nation: Five Years of Growth in Online Learning.* Needham, Mass.: Sloan Consortium, 2007.

Betts, J. R., and McFarland, L. L. "Safe Port in a Storm: The Impact of Labor Market Conditions on Community College Enrollments." *Journal of Human Resources*, 1995, *30*(4), 741–765.

Bitner, M. J., Ostrom, A.L., and Meuter, M. L. "Implementing Successful Self-Service Technologies." *Academy of Management Executives*, 2002, *16* (November), 26–40.

Borden, V. M. H. "Analysis Has Its Limitations." *Community College Week*, November 30, 2008.

Bushong, S. "Community College Enrollments Are Up, but Institutions Struggle to Pay for Them." *Chronicle of Higher Education*, January 23, 2009.

Cohen, A. M., and Brawer, F. B. *The American Community College.* (5th Ed). San Francisco: Jossey-Bass, 2008.

Carnevale, A., Smith, N., and Strohl, J. *Help Wanted: Projections of Jobs and Education Requirements Through 2018.* Washington, D.C.: Georgetown University Center on Education and the Workforce, 2010.

Carr, C. "Managing the Enrollment Boom." *Community College Journal*, 2009, *80*(1), 22–25.

Castor, D., Atkinson, R., and Ezell, S. *Embracing the Self-Service Economy.* Washington, D.C.: Information Technology & Innovation Foundation, 2010.

Center for Community College Student Engagement. *Making Connections: Dimensions of Student Engagement (2009 CCSSE Findings).* Austin: University of Texas at Austin, 2009.

Gabe, G. "Bounce Rate and Exit Rate, What Is the Difference and Why You Should Care." 2007. Retrieved June 10, 2010, from http://www.hmtweb.com/blog/2007/08/bounce-rate-and-exit-rate-what-is.html.

Gumport, P. J., and Pusser, B.M. "Restructuring the Academic Environment." In *Planning and Management for a Changing Environment.* pp. 452–478. San Francisco: Jossey-Bass, 1997.

Levin, J. S. "The Business Culture of the Community College: Students as Consumers; Students as Commodities." In B. Pusser (ed.), *Arenas of Entrepreneurship: Where Non-Profit and For-Profit Institutions Compete.* New Directions for Higher Education, 129, San Francisco: Jossey-Bass, 2005.

Li, C., and Bernoff, J. *Groundswell: Winning in a World Transformed by Social Technologies.* Boston: Harvard Business Press, 2008.

Shu-Hsun, H., and Ying-Yin, K. "Effects of Self-Service Technology on Customer Value and Customer Readiness: The Case of Internet Banking." *Internet Research*, 2008, *18*(4), 427–446.

Spool, J. M. "The $300 Million Button." 2009. Retrieved May 11, 2009, from http://www.uie.com/articles/three_hund_million_button/.

Virginia Community College System. "Dateline 2009." 2003. Retrieved June 6, 2010, from http://vccs.edu/ChancellorsDatelineVision/tabid/426/Default.aspx.

Zeithaml, V., Bitner, M. J., and Gremler, D. D. *Services Marketing*, 5th Ed. New York: Irwin/McGraw-Hill, 2009.

M. CRAIG HERNDON *is the special assistant to the chancellor for the Virginia Community College System in Richmond, VA.*

3

Little attention has been paid to the practical implications of implementing a unit record system on a community college campus. Potential benefits include the ability to capture student success and track outcomes for external compliance and internal planning efforts, but potential issues could impact the ability of a community college to manage the implementation of a system, including privacy, security, dealing with students who opt out, integration with current systems, data verification, and agency coordination. This chapter addresses the challenges and opportunities of implementing a unit record system on campus by addressing potential costs, benefits, and integration with already existing data and accountability processes.

Practical Implications of Implementing a Unit Record System on a Community College Campus

Joe Offermann, Ryan Smith

In 1938, Coleman Griffith wrote an article about the value of using research in decision making in higher education, warning that "the difficulty may not lie with the data at all, [but] in a complete failure to use the data as a means to an end, the end being thoroughly educational in intent and outcome" (p. 248). Over seventy years later, colleges and universities are struggling with issues related to using evidence in decision making, with accountability putting a new twist on an old problem.

The contemporary community college is currently witnessing significant transformations of what it means to be accountable and how accountability and quality improvement efforts overlap. Community colleges are increasingly responding to calls for accountability by shifting from a focus on access and enrollment to a focus on outcomes and student success (Bailey and Morest, 2006). In addition, many community colleges are

NEW DIRECTIONS FOR COMMUNITY COLLEGES, no. 154, Summer 2011 © 2011 Wiley Periodicals, Inc.
Published online in Wiley Online Library (wileyonlinelibrary.com) • DOI: 10.1002/cc.444

31

embracing improvement strategies that emphasize the use of data in decision making, as demonstrated by initiatives like Achieving the Dream or
the American Association of Community College's Completion Challenge
(Allen and Kazis, 2007). Both of the transformations, while different in
their purpose and audience, address one particular problem: providing
decision makers with information about the performance and effectiveness
of community colleges and enhancing the ability to make decisions based
on evidence.

A popular solution that addresses both accountability and improvement is the unit record system, also known as a longitudinal data system or
longitudinal database. A longitudinal data system organizes data in a way
that allows students to be tracked throughout their educational career in
one central location, generally from elementary school all the way through
completion of a bachelor's degree. The unit record system accomplishes this
by identifying specific points of progression in preschool, secondary, and
postsecondary education, including teachers, completions along the way,
and social, economic, and other demographic information about students.
Because data are organized around students as opposed to around the institutions, advocates of unit record systems assert that colleges and policy
makers can identify and more easily control for student and institutional
characteristics that enhance or inhibit student success. Critics cite concerns
about privacy, redundancy, necessity, and burden, and question whether
a longitudinal data system is worth the large investment of time and
resources.

Although unit record systems have been the subject of considerable
discussion among institutions and state agendas for higher education, there
has been little examination of the practical implications of implementing
them on a community college campus. As with most accountability efforts
aimed at meeting simultaneously the ends of accountability and quality
improvement, implementation can break down when policy makers and
those on campuses operate under different assumptions about what it
means to be accountable and how evidence is used in decision making
(Julian and Smith, 2007).

In order to identify the benefits and potential shortcomings of unit
record system implementation on a campus, it is helpful to know the context in terms of how community colleges use evidence in decision making
and what the elements of a unit record system are. The problem, after all,
is not what technology to use but rather "how we should restructure
higher education institutions to be effective 21st-century organizations"
(Johnstone, 2007, p. xi). The technology behind a solution like a unit
record system is only as good as the organizational culture, structure, and
resources that support it. This chapter examines issues related to the implementation of a unit record system by discussing the use of evidence in decision making, differences in approaches by community colleges and policy
makers, and the pros and cons of implementing such a system.

Using Data in Decision Making

Community colleges collect and have access to a multitude of data from a wide variety of sources. There is a lack of consensus, however, on how well community colleges—and education institutions in general—use data in decision making. The lack of consensus is largely a result of dynamics inherent internally to community colleges and other dynamics that exist externally in the community college environment.

Internal Dynamics. Educators in general state that they do use data in decision making on a regular basis but that barriers such as political considerations, organizational culture or governance dynamics, time, and resources can impede their use (Firnberg and Lasher, 1983; Nelson, Leffler, and Hansen, 2009). Additional barriers that might impede the use of evidence in decision making include the unique organizational structure and mission of the community college, unrecognized differences between espoused values and those that can be explained by behavior, and organizational perceptions about knowledge and how it should be applied.

Organizational Structure. A significant barrier to the use of evidence in decision making for community colleges is their mission and organizational structure. Between 1965 and 2000, the number of community colleges in the United States nearly tripled, while enrollment increased by about 475 percent, compared to 104 percent at four-year institutions (Phillippe and Sullivan, 2005). In the process of accommodating rapid growth, many community colleges established horizontal structures and isolated units—hallmarks of bureaucracies—to manage program growth and competing demands by students, governments, and other stakeholders. According to Birnbaum (1988), "as the number of subunits [in a bureaucracy] increase, [they] become increasingly specialized, and structures become more complex. Interaction decreases, more structured means of interaction are required, and the institution becomes bureaucratized" (pp. 106–107).

Coupled with increased demands for accountability and associated reporting requirements, the end result was data systems constructed around bureaucratic processes and accountability measures that may not reflect the reality of community college students' enrollment patterns or how students succeed. Other central elements of the community college that make up a significant portion of enrollment and revenues, such as workforce development, contract training, adult education, and other noncredit areas, may even utilize different data systems or standards. The nature of community college students, who exhibit complex enrollment patterns such as swirl or reverse transfer, means that crucial data can be lost at specific points (Hebel, 2008; McCormick, 2003). Additionally, community colleges generally are focused on local needs and thus must expend time and effort on contextualizing data. As a result, community college data systems capture a lot of information about the institution but can have difficulty capturing the nature of student enrollments or outcomes.

NEW DIRECTIONS FOR COMMUNITY COLLEGES • DOI: 10.1002/cc

Espoused Theories and Theories in Use. An additional internal barrier is the difference between declarative statements and action. Tagg (2003) investigated the reasons why organizations that purport to exist to enhance student learning end up "mired in bureaucracy, buried in regulations, hampered by apathy, or limited by resources" (p. 12). Using research from Argyris and Schon (1975), the author explains that organizations, like people, operate under two divergent theories of action: espoused and in use. Espoused theories are theories that people and organizations articulate in everyday conversations, presentations, meetings, goal and mission statements, and other forms of communication. In-use theories, however, are those that can be inferred through action (Tagg, 2003). Espoused theories are the most visible and are articulated in mission and core value statements. Therefore, most people are aware of their existence and place value on them. In-use theories actually can be inferred through behavior. People are unaware of in-use theories, however, because they are not articulated and there is no language associated with them. This phenomenon is the central claim of critics of community colleges, who "argue that community colleges uphold only in word, and vitiate in practice, the ideal of equality of opportunity" (Dougherty, 1994, p. 18).

The result of this approach, according to Tagg (1998), is that processes such as offering courses, providing student services, giving grades, constructing buildings, and printing transcripts are elevated to the level of actual mission, even though one would be hard-pressed to find a community college that actually would declare growing enrollment or the construction of buildings as its mission. Similarly, Alfred (2005) also observed that many institutions elevate declarative statements to the level of mission. These statements may describe intent but are not tied to actual operations; thus, interest in them "wanes and units begin to operate independently, sometimes at cross purposes" (p. 13). So, although a college purports to exist to meet the learning needs of students, in actuality it exists to offer a set of well-meaning but disconnected courses and services that only incidentally interact with each other and may or may not lead to learning.

Using Knowledge in Decision Making. A third internal dynamic that makes the use of evidence in decision making problematic are assumptions about knowledge and its use. Pfeffer and Sutton (2000, 2006), who have written extensively about using knowledge in decision making, cite several reasons for why efforts at using evidence in decision making often fail These reasons include the political and organizational risk of data revealing unpopular evidence; a vast amount of conflicting and contradictory conclusions; an overreliance on formal systems that fail to capture tacit knowledge acquired through organizational history, stories, and context; and an emphasis on the lure of technology and coding of data over synthesis and evaluation.

External Dynamics. Externally, a significant barrier to using evidence in decision making is inconsistency among policy organizations, accreditation agencies, state and federal governments, and internal data requests by specific programs in terms of requirements and expectations. Navigating the complex web of state and federal mandates, consortium agreements, national and regional policy initiatives, accreditation requirements, internal ad hoc requests, and local data needs requires an extensive amount of time and coordination—a luxury many community colleges do not have. Often many external entities are looking for the same answers, but the nature of the question may be different enough to require answering it multiple times to fit narrow needs. Not only do the multiple and various reporting requirements increase reporting burdens and take away time from priority data needs, but it makes it difficult for community colleges to tailor specific evidence for use in making decisions.

At Joliet Junior College in Joliet, IL, for instance, regular reports are required for submission to the institutional accreditation agency, the Higher Learning Commission (HLC). Participation in the Academic Quality Improvement Program through HLC requires another level of coordination and analysis. Similar reports are submitted to the Illinois Community College Board, the U.S. Department of Education through the Integrated Postsecondary Education Data System, and the Illinois Student Aid Commission. Consortium agreements with the South Metropolitan Higher Education Consortium and other institutional entities provide another level of data that must be presented in a regional context. Data collection and analysis also must meet state standards for dual credit programs with high schools. In order to meet the American College and University Presidents' Climate Commitment, the college must gather years of historical data and reports from a variety of departments. Data standards, reporting requirements, and best practices also exist in human resource, budgeting, facilities, and sustainability functions. This list highlights the complexity of multiple databases and requirements that community colleges must comply with.

View from the Community College Campus

Although variability exists in how community colleges use data, community colleges in general collect, store, and analyze data at the institutional, program, and external levels.

Institutional-Level Data. Most of the information at the institutional level is collected and stored on campus information systems as part of a college's enterprise resource plan (ERP). ERPs generally include a wide variety of student academic and demographic information, in addition to human resource, financial, and other operational processes. Most community colleges also have volumes of information about their students gathered through surveys, such as the Community College Survey of Student Engagement or in-house occupational follow-up, graduate, or satisfaction surveys. In general, institutional research and information technology offices act as stewards of this information. Due to staff expertise in data collection, stewardship, research techniques, and evaluation, these offices often are required to conduct a variety of analyses.

Program-Level Data. Extensive data also exist at the programmatic level and often can be linked to data at the institutional level. Deans and directors generally use program-level data in program review, evaluation, accreditation, and budgeting, and work with institutional research or information technology departments if the data needs to be triangulated with data that exist in ERPs. Noncredit areas, in general, have been particularly problematic in that there is usually disparate, or even no, external account-ability reporting requirements. Even if data reporting or tracking exists, the systems and reporting requirements are generally separate from other reporting and accountability requirements, inhibiting access and use by community colleges (Mullins and Lebesch, 2010). Thus, it is difficult to track or evaluate the effectiveness of programs in adult education, contract training, workforce development, or personal enrichment that nearly all community colleges offer.

External Data. Many external data sources also provide valuable information to community colleges (Stevens, 2008), but access and the ability to triangulate with institutional data systems can be problematic. In order to gain information about the success of transfer students, many community colleges use the National Student Loan Clearinghouse (NSLC) or rely on the goodwill of senior institutions to provide information or reports about transfer students. In regard to labor market databases, community colleges often rely on state labor market, workforce, or other employment systems. An example of this type of analysis is an economic impact study for community colleges in Illinois. Conducted by Northern Illinois University in conjunction with individual campuses, the study matched institutional-level data with state-level earnings, residency, migration, and occupational data from the Illinois Department of Employment Security from over a ten-year period (Northern Illinois University, 2007).

View from Policy Makers

Over the last decade, policy makers have asserted that unit record systems can act as a remedy by simultaneously demonstrating accountability and creating a culture of evidence (Basken, 2010; Burd, 2006; Fischer, 2006). Thus, it is no surprise that activism in the area has increased and that data systems have grown and become more sophisticated in their organization and elements.

Federal, State, and National Activism. Unit record systems have been a crucial element of educational reform movements of the last decade. The federal government has become increasingly active in the last decade, as evidenced by the data requirements of the No Child Left Behind legislation (Ewell and Boeke, 2007), the Education's Grant Program for Statewide Longitudinal Data Systems (Government Accountability Office, 2010), and the U.S. Department of Education's proposed student record system (Cunningham, Milam, and Statham, 2005). The National Commission on Accountability and the secretary of education's commission on the future of higher education have also placed emphasis on a student record system as a key component of accountability and enhancing quality (Burd, 2006; National Commission on Accountability in Higher Education, 2005). And panels discussing the topic through the National Commission on Accountability and the secretary of education's Commission on the Future of Higher Education (Burd, 2006; National Commission on Accountability in Higher Education, 2005).

Activism varies by state but has grown significantly in the last decade. A 2002 analysis by Dougherty (2002) identified fifteen states as possessing the ability to match student records. Another 2002 survey by Ewell, Schild, and Paulson (2003) discovered that thirty-nine states operate forty-six student unit record systems, with some states possessing multiple systems. The authors estimated that about 86 percent of all full-time undergraduates are covered by some kind of student unit record system and that most data systems only cover public institutions within the state. A 2006 survey by Ewell and Boeke (2007) showed that all but ten states had a student unit record system.

According to the Data Quality Campaign (2010), fifty states possess a unique student identifier to connect students across databases and years, thirty-three have the ability to match records—for students from pre-school all the way through 12th grade, twenty-four have the ability to match students with teachers, and twenty-three can aggregate data at the transcript level. Nearly every state now has at least one element of a longitudinal data system in place.

Organization of Unit Record Systems. According to the National Center for Higher Education Management Systems (NCHEMS; 2005, most state student unit record systems are organized as relational databases, data warehouses, or flat text files. Generally, schools and postsecondary institutions submit information to an entity in a prescribed data format. Most states also utilize a third party as a steward of the data. Rules governing the use of the data are generally defined by legislative mandate, coordinating agency policy, or agreed-on rules and protocols among individual institutions (NCHEMS, 2005). Generally, these agencies provide guidance on the contents of the data systems, set governing rules, and evaluate the system.

Elements of Longitudinal Databases. Several authors have outlined the elements of student unit record systems. Two studies noted that most databases capture term-level data; use the Social Security number as a unique identifier; and capture elements related to demographic, academic background, enrollment status, academic activity, and academic achievement (Ewell and Boeke, 2007; Ewell et al., 2003). The Florida PK20 Education Data Warehouse includes information about student demographics, test scores, financial aid, and employment, along with information about the educational institutions attended and faculty and staff data, including instructional activities and demographics (Florida Department of Education, n.d.).

Potential Benefits of Implementing a Unit Record System on Campus

Demonstrating Effectiveness and Accountability. Demonstrating effectiveness in a community college setting is problematic because the linkages between what happens before and after a student's experience in a community college are muddled at best. Many students entering a community college are underprepared, and, due to the open enrollment mission, many community colleges have imperfect information about student preparation. Graduation surveys and linkages to labor market and NSLC data may provide some good information about outcomes but do not tell the entire story. Thus, a longitudinal data system can provide critical information about institutional effectiveness and demonstrate accountability.

An example of a benefit from a unit record system for a community college would be the identification of successful outcomes linked to course or competency completions as opposed to credentials. An economic impact study by Northern Illinois University , for instance, found that Illinois community college students who do not complete a credential receive an extra $226 in annual earnings for each credit hour earned (Northern Illinois University, 2007). A longitudinal data system also could capture successful outcomes related to workforce development by clarifying how noncredit courses and programs directly lead to specific transitions, such as to a specific labor market or credit-based academic program (Government Accountability Office, 2004).

Enhancing Decision Making. When queried as to why many organizations struggle with using evidence in decision making, Peter Drucker, an influential management consultant and expert in human capital development, stated: "Thinking is very hard work. And management fashions are a wonderful substitute for thinking" (as quoted in Pfeffer and Sutton, 2006, p. 219). Implementing, maintaining, and using the information from a unit record system will likely be hard work and require an extensive amount of analysis, but the systems have the potential to highlight areas of improvement and build on the strengths that are hallmarks of community colleges, like access, responsiveness to community needs, and offering programming in credit and non-credit areas. By their nature, unit record systems also require an extensive amount of input from multiple internal departments. This input could enhance collaboration across the college and put the focus on the issue or problem revealed by the data, as opposed to putting the focus of the problem on a department or individual.

Advocacy. Advocacy in community colleges has a quantitative and qualitative nature. Unit record systems have the potential to facilitate dialog between postsecondary institutions and employers about student needs and success rates. A GAO (2010) study noted a situation where the State of Florida was able to communicate to an industry interested in relocating to the state the educational attainment level of a particular group of employees, while Indiana used the information to inform regional economic development entities about the educational attainment of citizens for a specific region. From a qualitative perspective, a unit record system can clarify how issues of social class, like first-generation status, are woven into the lives of community colleges colleges and their impact on student success. In that regard, unit record systems can help policy makers and administrators understand not only the cost of programs and services, but also their value.

Ability to Connect with Other Sectors. Unit record systems also could provide a forum for community colleges and secondary schools to develop curricula that enhance the preparedness of entering students, with each sector identifying areas of success and areas that need improvement. On the outcomes end, for example, data systems could be linked with transfer and labor market outcomes, such as transfer and labor market outcomes, providing further connections among community colleges and four-year institutions and local business and industry.

A student unit record system also could change the language currently associated with accountability movements. Sectors do not act in isolation; holding a community college solely responsible for the success or failure of a student when so many other factors play a role is unreasonable. A unit record system also could shift the language to one based on successes, as opposed to the high-stakes "pass-fail, succeed-fail" language that dominates K–12 and, increasingly, higher education accountability efforts (Fine, 2008).

Potential Issues Associated with Implementing a Unit Record System on Campus

Burden. A significant challenge lies in the burden placed on community colleges in the implementation stage. A study by the National Center for Education Statistics identified two types of potential burdens that could be placed on colleges, one associated with initial implementation and the other with subsequent reporting (Cunningham and others, 2005). Implementation burdens include upgrades for existing software, technology conversions, initial training, and integration of historical data files. Reporting burdens include dealing with missing or mismatched records, changes in student records, and increased labor demands, although some institutional researchers involved in the report stated that labor costs could be offset by the benefits derived from the system.

Privacy Issues. Another challenge are privacy laws, such as the Family Educational Rights and Privacy Act (FERPA), that limit the type of data that can be shared and reported (Cunningham and others, 2005; Ewell and Jenkins, 2008). Concerns have been raised about how unit record systems expose data about students and other individuals to other sectors. Currently, federal legislation supports state activism in implementing longitudinal data systems (Winnick, Palmer, and Coleman, 2007). Community colleges would need to ensure that their data systems are consistent and compliant with state and federal laws and guidelines, such as the FERPA.

Redundancy and Integration.   Another potential limitation at the campus level is redundancy. Today, community colleges have access to an unprecedented level of sophistical analysis tools and generally are accustomed to conducting analyses that link disparate data systems (Bers, 2008). Policy makers need to ensure that the implementation of a unit record system on a community college campus does not exceed a standard that is already being met. Along those lines, policy makers need to acknowledge the fact of variability of data systems and ERPs among community colleges.

Use of Information and Results.   Many unit record systems, and accountability efforts in general, place a strong emphasis on variables over which community colleges have limited control: high schools, teachers, and demographic data, for instance. Adelman (2005) points out that "even when these variables prove to be statistically significant, shy of aggressive, targeted recruitment there is nothing a community can do to change them in order to produce less differential results" (p. 119). When there is a lack of clarity of goals or consensus on the purpose of a unit record system, community colleges could divert to the selection of variables that are the most convenient, as opposed to ones that enhance decision making or student learning.

Trust.   A final issue that may be problematic in integrating a unit record system on a community college campus is trust. Johnstone (2007) discusses this phenomenon in her excellent book about the use of technology in higher education, noting that while technology has the power to create intellectual capital and enhance campus efficiencies, it also can create a sense of disillusionment, as individuals are further disconnected from real and direct contact with other people and processes. Johnstone further notes that this creates new demands on leaders and governance structures, demands that have yet to be further explored or analyzed. Policy makers will need to spend a lot of time up front building trust and explaining the rationale behind the implementation of a unit record system. Community college leaders will need to do the same on their campus when articulating the reasons behind and value of a unit record system to faculty and to information technology and institutional research staff.

Practical Implications of Implementing a Longitudinal Data System

Community college leaders can take several steps to ensure that a longitudinal data system will be used to meet the dual needs of institutional improvement and accountability by enhancing decision making.

Assign Responsibility. Responsibility must be assigned to someone who possesses a high level of technical expertise but is also adept at building positive internal relationships based on trust and doing what is best for the college. This person also should act as the institutional expert and liaison with external agencies.

Incorporate Unit Record System Processes and Results into Governance, Operational, and Planning Structures. Community colleges should resist the temptation to view a unit record system as an innovation, something that is outside the boundaries of normal organizational governance and decision-making processes, or as another compliance effort. New innovations by themselves are not bad, but it is difficult for them to compete for scarce resources or with traditional structures developed over decades or that continue by momentum. In fact, when an innovation stumbles, blame usually is placed on politics or administration but rarely on the innovation's practical value (Curry, 1992). Ultimately, innovations fail because they are "by definition departures from traditional organizational practices [with a] somewhat different set of goals, norms, and values, and, as a result, different set of boundaries" (Levine, 1980, p. 13). For a unit record system to be used and valued, it must be incorporated into institutional governance, operational, and planning efforts.

Pay Attention to Privacy. Community colleges also should ensure privacy and confidentiality to external and internal groups. Students, parents, and community members want to know their community college is doing a good job but also want to know that it can be trusted and cares about what matters to them. In this case, there would be a lot of value in training and in clarifying FERPA and privacy rules (Ewell and Boeke, 2007).

Be Genuine, Not Just Transparent. Community colleges should place more focus on being genuine with the data as opposed to being transparent. In Douglas Adams' comedy/science fiction novel *The Hitchhiker's Guide to the Galaxy* (1979) the author relates a story about a race of aliens bent on destroying Earth to make way for an intergalactic highway, with humans given a two-minute warning to evacuate. Earth's inhabitants understandably protest but are met with this response from the aliens:

> There's no point in acting surprised about it. All the planning charts and demolition orders have been on display at your local planning department in Alpha Centauri for 50 of your Earth years, so you've had plenty of time to lodge any formal complaint and it's far too late to start making a fuss about it now. . . . What do you mean you've never been to Alpha Centauri? Oh, for heaven's sake, mankind, it's only four light years away, you know. I'm sorry, but if you can't be bothered to take an interest in local affairs, that's your own lookout. Energize the demolition beams. (p. 26).

The temptation with improvement and accountability efforts is to place them on a Web site or deliver in a report without any context or narrative. Although doing so certainly is transparent, it is hardly genuine. Community colleges should celebrate the strengths that the results of a longitudinal data system will show and be honest about areas for improvement. No one expects any college to be perfect, but they do expect a college to state how it is going to improve in areas that need improvement.

Avoid Duplication and Redundancy. Community colleges should advocate for reporting the same information to multiple agencies. The results from a longitudinal data system can be used to fulfill multiple state, federal, accreditation, and program accountability requirements. Community colleges should advocate for a more streamlined accountability system that can meet all of these requirements. State coordinating agencies, the U.S. Department of Education, and accreditation agencies should all work together to ensure consistent reporting requirements that will help community colleges spend more time on analysis and use of the data and less time on compliance.

Use the System as a Vehicle for Changing the Culture. Finally, remember that the successful implementation and use of a longitudinal data system does not lie in the technological implementation of the system but rather in its impact in helping students achieve their academic goals. Data systems and processes, by themselves, cannot dream, think, be creative, or implement change. Only people can dream, think, be creative, and implement change. As Anandam (1998) states, "[I]t is not a question of competence but a question of cultural change" (p. 89).

Conclusion

In writing about evidence and accountability, Douglas Harris (2010) points out that "if we have to prove beyond a reasonable doubt that something new will be better, then the status quo will reign forever" (p. 36). Community colleges should approach unit record systems with an open mind but clearly communicate and understand the benefits and limitations associated with them. Community colleges and policy makers would be wise to head the words of Coleman Griffith seventy years ago and realize that the difficulty does not "lie with the data at all" but in tapping into the human capacity to use it for change and intentionality.

References

Adams, D. *The Ultimate Hitchhiker's Guide to the Galaxy.* New York: Del Ray, 2002.
Adelman, C. *Moving Into Town and Moving On: The Community College in the Lives of Traditional-age Students.* Washington, D.C.: U.S. Department of Education, 2005.
Alfred, R. Managing the Big Picture in Colleges and Universities: From Tactics to Strategy. Lanham, Md.: Rowman and Littlefield, 2005.
Allen, L., and Kazis, R. *Building a Culture of Evidence in Community Colleges.* Boston: Jobs for the Future, 2007.

Anandam, K. "A Call for Action." In K. Anandam (ed.), *Integrating Technology on Campus*. San Francisco: Jossey-Bass, 1998.

Argyris, C., and Schon, D. A. *Theory in Practice*. San Francisco: Jossey-Bass, 1975.

Bailey, T., and Morest, V. S. "Introduction." In T. Bailey and V. S. Morest (eds.), *Defending the Community College Equity Agenda*. Baltimore, Md.: Johns Hopkins University Press, 2006.

Basken, P. "States Embrace Student-Data Tracking, with Prodding from White House." *Chronicle of Higher Education*, January 3, 2010. Retrieved May 1, 2010, from http://chronicle.com/article/States-Embrace-Student-Data/63376/.

Bers, T. "Editor's Notes." In T. Bers (ed.), *Student Tracking in the Community College*. San Francisco: Jossey-Bass, 2008.

Birnbaum, R. *How Colleges Work*. San Francisco: Jossey-Bass, 1988.

Burd, S. "Spellings Seeks Allies for Unit-Record System." *Chronicle of Higher Education*, November 24, 2006, p. A31.

Cunningham, A. F., Milam, J., and Statham, C. *Feasibility of a Student Unit Record System Within the Integrated Postsecondary Education Data System*. Washington, D.C.: National Center for Education Statistics, March 2005.

Curry, B. K. *Instituting Enduring Innovations: Achieving Continuity of Change in Higher Education*. Washington, D.C.: George Washington University, 1992.

Data Quality Campaign. "Inaugural Overview of States' Actions to Leverage Data to Improve Student Success." 2010. Retrieved May 1, 2010, from http://www.dataqualitycampaign.org/resources/846.

Dougherty, C. *A Policymaker's Guide to the Value of Longitudinal Student Data*. Boulder, Colo.: Education Commission of the States, 2002.

Dougherty, K. J. *The Contradictory College*. Albany: State University of New York, 1994.

Ewell, P., and Boeke, M. *Critical Connections: Linking States' Unit Record Systems to Track Student Progress*. Indianapolis, Ind.: Lumina Foundation, 2007.

Ewell, P., and Jenkins, D. "Using State Student Unit Record Data to Increase Community College Student Success." In T. Bers (ed.), *Student Tracking in the Community College*. San Francisco: Jossey-Bass, 2008.

Ewell, P., Schild, P.R., and Paulson, K. *Following the Mobile Student*. Indianapolis, Ind.: Lumina Foundation, 2003.

Fine. S. M. "Consumed by Failure: Shifting the Language of School Accountability." *Education Week*, March 18, 2008, p. 22.

Firnberg, J. W., and Lasher, W. F. (eds.). *Politics and Pragmatics of Institutional Research*. San Francisco: Jossey-Bass, 1983.

Fischer, K. "Accountability Panel Says Government Should Collect More Data on Students." *Chronicle of Higher Education*, March 16, 2006, p. A25.

Florida Department of Education. "PK20 Education Data Warehouse Fact Sheet." Retrieved June 11, 2010, from http://edwapp.doe.state.fl.us/EDW_Facts.htm.

Government Accountability Office. *Public Community and Technical Schools: Most Schools Use Both Credit and Noncredit Programs for Workforce Development*. Washington, D.C.: Government Accountability Office, 2004.

Government Accountability Office. *Postsecondary Education: Most States Collect Graduates'Employment Information, but Clearer Guidance on Student Privacy Requirements Is Needed*. Washington, D.C.: Government Accountability Office, 2010.

Griffith, C. R. "Functions of a Bureau of Institutional Research." *Journal of Higher Education*, 1938, 9(5), 248–255.

Harris, D. "The Evidence on the Race to the Top." *Education Week*, March 31, 2010, p. 36.

Hebel, S. "News Analysis: Higher Education's Grade for Data 'Incomplete.'" *Chronicle of Higher Education*, December 5, 2008. Retrieved May 1, 2010, from http://chronicle.com/article/Higher-Educations-Grade-fo/1387/.

Johnstone, S. *Advancing Campus Efficiencies*. Bolton, Mass.: Anker, 2006.

Julian, J., and Smith. R. "Accountability in Community Colleges." *On Research and Leadership Update*, 18, 2007. Retrieved May 1, 2010, from http://occrl.illinois.edu/Newsletter/2007/spring/3.

Levine, A. *Why Innovation Fails: The Institutionalization and Termination of Innovation in Higher Education.* Albany: State University of New York, 1980.

McCormick, A. C. "Swirling and Double-Dipping: New Patterns of Student Attendance and Their Implications for Higher Education." In J. E. King, E. L. Anderson, and M. E. Corrigan (eds.), *Changing Student Attendance Patterns.* San Francisco: Jossey-Bass, 2003.

Mullins, C. M., and Lebesch, A. *Moving Success from the Shadows: Data Systems that Link Education and Workforce Outcomes.* Washington, D.C.: American Association of Community Colleges, 2010.

National Center for Higher Education Management Systems. "Harnessing the Potential for Research of Existing Student Records Databases," 2005. Retrieved May 1, 2010, from http://www.dataqualitycampaign.org/resources/31.

Nelson, S. R., Leffler, J. C., and Hansen, B. A. *Toward a Research Agenda for Understanding and Improving the Use of Research Evidence.* Portland, Oreg.: Northwest Regional Educational Laboratory, 2009.

National Commission on Accountability in Higher Education. *Accountability for Better Results: A National Imperative for Higher Education.* Boulder, Colo.: State Higher Education Executive Officers, 2005.

Northern Illinois University. "The Economic Impact of Illinois Community Colleges: A Report to the Illinois Community College Board." Dekalb, Ill.: Center for Governmental Studies, 2007.

Pfeffer, J., and Sutton, R. *The Knowing-Doing Gap: How Smart Companies Turn Knowledge into Action.* Boston: Harvard Business School, 2000.

Pfeffer, J., and Sutton, R. *Hard Facts, Dangerous Half-Truths, and Total Nonsense: Profiting from Evidence-based Management.* Boston: Harvard Business School, 2006.

Phillippe, K., and Sullivan, L. *National Profile of Community Colleges: Trends and Statistics.* Washington, D.C.: American Association of Community Colleges, 2005.

Stevens, D. "Beyond Higher Education: Other Sources of Data for Tracking Students." In T. Bers (ed.), *Student Tracking in the Community College.* San Francisco: Jossey-Bass, 2008.

Tagg, J. *The Learning College Paradigm.* Bolton, Mass.: Anker, 2003.

Winnick, S., Palmer, S., and Coleman, A. *Maximizing the Power of Education Data while Ensuring Compliance with Federal Student Privacy Laws.* Washington, D.C.: Data Quality Campaign, 2007.

JOE OFFERMANN *is the director of institutional research and effectiveness at Joliet Junior College, Joliet, IL.*

RYAN SMITH *is the director of university assessment at Illinois State University, Normal, IL,*

4

Community colleges are known for keeping abreast of the latest instructional technologies, but the constant and rapid growth of available technology also presents challenges. This chapter reviews the current literature regarding instructional technology usage, with a focus on beneficial applications of technology for teaching and learning, and associated financial, managerial, and planning challenges. The chapter concludes with strategies for research, adoption, implementation, and maintenance of instructional technologies to enhance teaching and learning.

Planning for Instructional Technology in the Classroom

Regina L. Garza Mitchell

The 1990s began an increasing emphasis on teaching with technology, in particular a push for fully online courses. Now more than a decade into the twenty-first century, however, we are still trying to figure out not only which technologies to use but how, when, and why to use them in the classroom. Perspectives on technology use range from Luddites who intentionally avoid technology to those who use the latest gadgets and software as soon as they are available. However, teaching and learning with technology ranked fourth in a study of the top ten issues of strategic important facing information technology professionals (Ingerman and Yang, 2010). Likewise, a survey of 303 faculty members at colleges and universities indicated that although a majority of faculty (88 percent) feel that technology is essential in the classroom and useful for students, the two biggest challenges to incorporating technology are lack of funding and not knowing how to use it properly (CDW-G, 2010). Universities and larger colleges may have faculty development centers that offer centralized training and

The author thanks Anthony Freds from Mid Michigan Community College, who was instrumental in helping shape the final version of this chapter.

planning for the use of instructional technology, but the majority of community colleges are rural institutions in which faculty development efforts are more likely to be run by an administrator without a staff (Eddy, 2007). Thus, the onus of figuring out how and when to use technology often falls on faculty members as individuals.

Relatively few faculty members know how to successfully incorporate technology to enhance student learning, and those who are interested may not have access to the training or equipment that would allow them to do so. The majority of community colleges lack formal professional development for faculty members (Eddy, 2007) that could provide training in appropriately incorporating technology into teaching and learning. Therefore, colleges must be intentional in planning for the use of instructional technology.

Planning Considerations

Oftentimes, issues in strategic planning occur when the intent of the plans do not match the actions taken during the implementation process. Careful attention to the planning process and consideration of the issues associated with implementing and developing instructional technology can help colleges be intentional in creating a map that defines why and how technology should be used for instructional purposes while avoiding associated pitfalls.

Define and Assess. Colleges implement instructional technology usage for a variety of reasons including improving efficiency, increasing cost effectiveness, expanding student markets, increasing enrollment capacities, and better preparing students for workplace environments (Mars and Ginter, 2007). The technology necessary to fulfill each purpose varies. Like many trends in higher education, many institutions struggle to keep up without always questioning if they should keep up, how they should keep up, or which trends work best to support institutional goals and culture. The first step, then, is to define instructional technology and its purpose.

Numerous definitions and assumptions about instructional technology exist. For instance, the purpose of the Instructional Technology Council (ITC), one of the American Association of Community College's twenty-four affiliated councils, is "to raise awareness about the benefits of distance learning, instructional telecommunications, and future needs and possibilities" (ITC, 2011, para. 2). In contrast, the Association for Educational Communications and Technology (AECT), a professional association of educators at all levels, states that its mission includes "promoting scholarship and best practices in the creation, use, and management of technologies for effective teaching and learning in a wide range of settings" (AECT, 2011). The two definitions have very different emphases. The ITC specifically lists distance learning and instructional telecommunications, and its conferences and professional development activities primarily focus on e-learning. AECT's publications and conferences focus on the design of instruction to incorporate technology into the teaching and learning process. On most college campuses, instructional technology tends to be thought of as the technology tools (e.g., clickers, learning management systems, iPods, iPads, etc.) instead of a process that involves planning, implementing, evaluating, and managing the use of technology to enhance teaching and learning. When planning for instructional technology, it is important to learn how it is perceived by stakeholders in the process to ensure that those involved in planning its use have similar understandings of what it is and how it should be approached.

One of the most common reasons for incorporating instructional technology is to improve student learning. Educause (2010), a nonprofit organization committed to advancing higher education through technology, compiles a yearly list of the top teaching and learning challenges through input from faculty, staff, and administrators at colleges and universities across the nation. Challenges for 2010 included:

- Creating learning environments that promote active learning, critical thinking, collaborative learning, and knowledge creation
- Developing twenty-first-century literacies among students and faculty (information, digital, and visual)
- Reaching and engaging today's learner
- Encouraging faculty adoption and innovation in teaching and learning with instructional technology
- Advancing innovation in teaching and learning (with technology) in an era of budget cuts

Items on this list align with existing challenges faced by many community colleges and can provide a starting point for determining the "how" and "why" of planning for instructional technology.

Once a definition of instructional technology has been established, it is important to assess the college's current and future IT needs, including technological infrastructures, professional development, and resources. When planning for instructional technology, information technology units and academic units often have different ideas about what is necessary, what is desired, and which approaches to implementation and training to take. Further, college faculty and administrators often make assumptions about how students use technology and how they expect it to be used in the classroom. Sometimes those assumptions are correct; other times they may be far-fetched, depending on an institution's location and demographics. Administrators and faculty in colleges also tend to make assumptions about students' expectations for instructional technology. To avoid costly mistakes, it is essential to conduct a needs assessment to determine a college's true needs in regard to instructional technology.

The assessment should address the needs and expectations of students, faculty, staff, and administrators and the existing resources and infrastructure.

The assessment should address economic factors, current technologies being used, and anticipated growth. In addition to surveys that can be analyzed quantitatively, qualitative aspects of instructional technology needs and expectations also should be considered. Planning members can conduct focus groups with faculty, staff, and students. A vice president at one community college took the qualitative approach one step further and invited input from all interested stakeholders in determining what technology should be included in a new building (Anthony Freds, personal communication, February 11, 2011). In a one-on-one conversation, participants were asked, "If you could have anything you want, the sky is the limit, what would it be?" The responses provided a greater idea of what faculty, staff, and students expected in the new building and of the college in general.

Results from the assessment should be used to make determinations about the purpose of instructional technology, which facets are most important, appropriate tools and technology, and how instructional technology fits in to existing structures. Defining an institutional purpose for using technology will help narrow the scope for those who feel overwhelmed by technology, and conducting a needs assessment will help prevent needless spending on software and hardware that do not work toward the defined purposes.

Learning Curve. Although the focus of instructional technology is on student learning, it is also important to plan for associated learning curves in becoming comfortable with using technology and understanding how to use it correctly. Much of the literature about the current generation of students indicates that traditional-age students (i.e., ages 18–21) have grown up with technology and that they want and expect it to be used in the classroom. However, characteristics applied to Millennial students tend to encompass those in the middle classes rather than lower-income students (Wilson, 2008), which comprise the majority of community college students. Further, fewer people with lower incomes tend to own desktop or laptop computers, have broadband Internet access, or own gadgets such as iPods or e-book readers (Jansen, 2010), facts that indicate that students from lower socioeconomic backgrounds may have different needs in regard to technology usage and training. Consideration will have to be given to the types of training and support that can be provided for students taking classes that integrate instructional technology.

Some faculty and staff members have an aversion to using technology because it is unfamiliar and therefore uncomfortable. Moving from expert to novice is not an easy transition to make; thus resistance occurs. Resisters to technology often claim that if their teaching methods already work, there is no need to change. Faculty members and administrators who take this stance deny themselves the opportunity for lifelong learning. The key, then, is to help educators see the use of technology as another opportunity to build on what they already know and to enhance their own learning as well as their students' (Merriam, Cafferella, and Baumgartner, 2006). Colleges with the resources to offer training should plan carefully for these sessions, and staff members from all areas should be invited to participate. Even those staff members who are not instructors may appreciate being included; it is essential for staff members who interact regularly with students to know what happens in the classroom.

One of the greatest barriers to participation in training activities is time. If people cannot see the benefit of learning how to use technology, they will not attend trainings. Faculty members, particularly those who are not comfortable with using technology, can be incredibly resistant to training for technology they think they will not use or do not need to use. Thus, it is important to approach training for technology use from an adult learning perspective. We can invite meaningful participation by making training relevant. In addition to showing how to use the technology, faculty members also should learn *why* instructional technology can be beneficial to themselves and their students. Sessions should be led using best practice techniques for adult learners, including active learning techniques. An assessment component also should be included in formal training sessions to help faculty members gauge whether the technology is actually enhancing teaching and learning.

Resources. A major issue faced by community colleges today is a lack of resources. Resources in this context include the technology itself (hardware and software), time, and budget. This lack emanates from the typically minimalist budgets from which colleges have to work. However, several questions must be asked regarding resources: How much time will it take to implement a new technology? How much time will it take to train students, staff, and faculty adequately? What funds are available to purchase new equipment? How will end users be trained? Who will do the training? What technology is already available? What new resources are needed to implement IT appropriately? Future needs also must be kept in mind in determining necessary resources.

Time is a factor that should be considered from multiple angles. The person or department responsible for training will have to consider the time it will take: to set up the hardware or software; to learn how to use the technology properly; to train staff, faculty, and students; and for maintenance and support. As mentioned, not all colleges have staff members dedicated to training (Eddy, 2007), so an additional consideration may include funding to bring in consultants for training or for purchasing documentation. Planning for resources also should include researching grants to assist in providing start-up funds for new instructional technology initiatives and investigating consortia memberships to benefit from a collective effort.

In planning for instructional technology, it is also helpful to consider what already may be in place. For example, is there a dedicated server for storing movie clips that are used in the classroom? Using existing technology can be a cost saver in some ways, but the age of existing technology

should also be considered. In some instances, it may be cheaper to purchase something new than to try to upgrade outdated equipment.

When a college is fortunate enough to invest in technology for the
classroom, it also has to allocate resources for training, updating, and maintaining hardware and software in future years. Not keeping up with changes
and updates can be detrimental to faculty use (Debolt, 2008). Overlooking
necessary upgrades and ignoring training sends a message that technology
is not important or necessary, and it creates a hurdle for faculty and students who attempt to continue using technology.

Finally, colleges must plan for growth and change in the rate of use of
instructional technology and the rapid pace of change in technological
innovations. For example, a common complaint among students who bring
laptops to class is a lack of electrical outlets. Colleges also may experience
bandwidth issues when more students (and faculty) bring wireless devices
to campus. Yet another area of consideration is classroom furniture. Best
practices in teaching and learning no longer call for the "sage on the stage"
method of teaching but encourage group work and mobility. Outdated
furniture may prohibit instructional technology in the classroom if it is
difficult to move desks or tables into new configurations. Ensuring that
technology is available in the classroom at all times rather than being
checked out before each session is also a consideration. A final consideration should be the ability for a system or structure to grow. What will happen in five or ten years when major shifts have once again occurred? It is
essential to plan with one eye on the future.

Recommendations. The issues discussed in this chapter are broad
and cover a number of areas essential to planning for instructional technology use. Regardless of whether planning is a formal or grassroots process,
there are several ways in which that process can be enhanced.

- *Get input from those on the front lines.* Include faculty members in planning sessions. For those institutions that have a centralized planning
  and budgeting process for instructional technology, faculty should be
  included in the decision-making process. Their input is necessary to
  balance how technology is used and the most appropriate ways to
  incorporate it into teaching and learning. Multiple disciplinary perspectives should be represented in order to gain the greatest input as to
  what is needed on a broad scale, perhaps even as a subcommittee
  focused specifically on instructional technology in the classroom.
- *Seek alternative solutions.* Although many colleges are fortunate enough
  to have an information technology department or a faculty development
  office that takes the lead on planning for instructional technology, in a
  number of institutions, there is little to no budget available for instructional technology. If computers and an Internet connection are available
  in the classroom, instructors can make use of a wide variety of free or
  nearly free Web 2.0 applications. Colleges also may wish to consider

working with other institutions to share the cost of technology purchases, maintenance, and support. Working in concert with other colleges may provide discounts on the purchase price of costlier items. Administrators and faculty members, alone or in partnership with other institutions, should investigate grant opportunities for implementing instructional technology. Grants often provide money for training and support in addition to purchasing equipment. Organizations such as the ITC   (http://www.itcnetwork.org/resources/grant-opportunities.html) provide lists of grant programs related to instructional technology.

- *Keep the learning in mind.* The rate of change for technology is astronomical, and it is easy to become overwhelmed by the sheer amount of available tools. It is important to consider *how* a technology might be used as opposed to how popular it is. The end goal for implementing instructional technology is student learning. First determine what your students need, and then seek suitable tools.

- *Make it worthwhile.* Many faculty and staff members would love to take part in professional development that is technology-based, but they simply do not have the time to do so. By setting aside paid professional development time, administrators can encourage teachers to participate in technology training. The provision of incentives becomes an essential issue of importance in technology planning. The issue of lack of motivation is something that needs to be examined when dealing with planning for technology. If faculty members are not motivated to use the technology they have, acquiring new technology will be a waste of resources as individuals will be unwilling to use it.

- *Try it before you buy it.* Pilot testing is an essential component of instructional technology implementation. Prior to rolling out a campus-wide initiative, take advantage of early adopters and ask them to participate in a pilot test. Pilot testing also can be a low-pressure way of engaging faculty who are resistant to technology efforts. Providing training and allowing access to tools early on may help ease fears associated with technology use. Pilot testing also will allow you to work out the majority of issues prior to engaging a large number of faculty, and it provides the opportunity to build community among faculty and staff members by inviting feedback about the tool and about best practice approaches to teaching and learning with technology.

Conclusion

Planning for instructional technology requires effort on the behalf of many units within a college. Planning should not be the sole purview of administrators; rather faculty, staff, and students all should be considered and included in the process. The greater the amount of input into the planning process, the more successful implementation will be.

NEW DIRECTIONS FOR COMMUNITY COLLEGES • DOI: 10.1002/cc

References

Association for Educational Communications and Technology. *What is AECT?* Bloomington, Ind.: AECT, 2011. Retrieved February 12, 2011 from http://www. aect.org/About/default.asp.

CDW-G. *CDW-G 2010 21st-Century Campus Report: Campus 2.0.* Vernon Hills, Ill.: CDW-G, 2010. Retrieved September 21, 2010, from http://newsroom.cdwg.com/ features/feature-07-19-10.html.

Debolt, D. "Colleges Struggle to Keep 'Smart' Classrooms Up to Date." *Chronicle of Higher Education*, 2008, *55*(8), A17.

Eddy, P. L. "Faculty Development in Rural Community Colleges." In P. L. Eddy and J. P. Murray (eds.), *Rural Community Colleges: Teaching, Learning, and Leading in the Heartland, New Directions for Community Colleges 137*, pp. 65–76. San Francisco: Jossey-Bass, 2007.

Educause. "Educause Top Teaching and Learning Challenges Project." 2010. Retrieved September 21, 2010, from http://tlchallenges09.ning.com/

Ingerman, B. L., and Yang, C. "The Top-Ten IT Issues, 2010." *Educause Review*, 2010 *45*(3), 46–60.

Instructional Technology Council. "About ITC." 2011. Retrieved January 17, 2011, from http://www.itcnetwork.org/about-itc.html.

Jansen, J. *The Better-Off Online.* Washington, D.C.: Pew Research Center, 2010. Retrieved February 21, 2011, from http://pewresearch.org/pubs/1809/internet-usage-higher-income-americans.

Mars, M. M., and Ginter, M. B. "Connecting Organizational Environments with the Instructional Technology Practices of Community College Faculty." *Community College Review*, 2007, *34* (4), 324–343.

Merriam, S. B., Caffarella, R., and Baumgartner, L. *Learning in Adulthood: A Comprehensive Guide* (3rd ed.). San Francisco: Jossey-Bass, 2006.

Wilson, J. L. "The Millennials: Getting to Know Our Current Generation of Students." *Mountain Rise, the International Journal of the Scholarship of Teaching and Learning*, 2008, *5*(1).

REGINA L. GARZA MITCHELL *is assistant professor in the Department of Education Leadership at Central Michigan University.*

5

*The current generation of new students, referred to as the
Millennial Generation, brings a new set of challenges to
the community college. The influx of these technologically
sophisticated students, who interact through the social
phenomenon of Web 2.0 technology, bring expectations
that may reshape institutions of higher learning. This
chapter provides an overview of Web 2.0 technologies and
considerations of their potential to transform the way
education is delivered. Long-held learning beliefs and
established educational strategies may need to be
redefined to incorporate the benefits of Web 2.0 and to
serve the educational needs of the Millennial Generation.*

Web 2.0 Technologies: Applications for Community Colleges

Susanne K. Bajt

Introduction

With the explosion of Web 2.0 technologies in higher education, increased
student engagement and active learning strategies have become particularly
relevant in today's learning environments. Classroom strategies that support this kind of learning are considered even more meaningful when
teaching Millennial Generation students, those who were born from 1982
to 1991 (Oblinger and Oblinger, 2005). Today's students have been
described as having an information age mind-set, being Millennials or
members of the Net Generation.

The technology and media used by children during their formative
years may very well have an influence on how they learn as well as on their
learning expectations. Millennial learners have different learning styles that
require faculty to reconsider pedagogical methods (Prensky, 2001). These

NEW DIRECTIONS FOR COMMUNITY COLLEGES, no. 154, Summer 2011 © 2011 Wiley Periodicals, Inc.
Published online in Wiley Online Library (wileyonlinelibrary.com) • DOI: 10.1002/cc.446

students embrace interactive environments, have different ways of thinking and communicating, and seek active involvement in their learning (Oblinger and Oblinger, 2005). Traditional classroom structures and teaching strategies may be ineffective due to the learning needs of these students who process information differently. Faculty must consider the impact of Millennial learning preferences for digital literacy, collaboration, experiential learning, and immediacy in both course design and delivery (Skiba and Barton, 2006). For example, by embedding Web-based interactions, tools, and applications within a course, Millennial Generation preferences may be supported.

Students from the Net Generation have grown up in a digital world and expect to use these tools to their advantage in learning environments. Prensky (2001) referred to these students as "digital natives" and suggested that they are the first generation to grow up immersed in technology. Millennials, accustomed to the multitasking, connected, and immediate-payoff world of their video games and online experiences, are bored by many of the educational methods and strategies used in today's classrooms. The many skills this generation has developed from new technologies, which may have a profound effect on their learning, are almost totally ignored by educators (Prensky, 2001). Richardson (2009) described the disparity between how the Millennial Generation and most faculty communicate: "The world is changing around us, yet as a system, we have been very, very slow to react. Our students' realities in terms of the way they communicate and learn are very different from our own" (5). Just as many of our brains have been retrained by television, the Millennials are retraining their brains in newer ways, some of which may be just the opposite to our ways of thinking (Prensky, 2001). Net Generation students almost instinctively connect to the Internet to seek immediate information. Students of this generation are naturally inclined to "focus on understanding, constructing knowledge using discovery methods and active engagement" (Brown, 2000, p. 4). They want faculty to provide them with guidance and a customized learning experience in the classroom. Meanwhile, the emergence of Web 2.0 tools, while offering many instructional opportunities, may have widened the gap between the use of technology by faculty and by students.

Significance of the Millennial Generation

As the current wave of one of the largest populations in the history of the United States, the Millennial Generation, permeates college campuses and the workplace, the need to understand them is imminent. This generation is one of the largest populations since the "baby boomers," representing over 30 percent of the population (Tapscott, 1998). This current generation of traditional-age college students has grown up with technology. Born between 1980 and 1994, the Millennials have been defined by Carlson

New Directions for Community Colleges • DOI: 10.1002/cc

(2005) as smart but impatient, wanting immediate results, and they expect to be able to choose how, where, and what they learn. America's first generation to exceed 100 million people, this generation brings a blend of attitudes, skills, and expectations that creates opportunities as well as challenges for academic institutions (Hartman, Moskal, and Dziuban, 2005).

The Millennial Generation, as the largest generation in our nation's history, holds important implications for how colleges develop programs (Coomes and DeBard, 2004). Between 1990 and 2004, the enrollment of undergraduate Millennial students increased by 31 percent; enrollment of adult college students increased by 17 percent during the same period. By 2012, the number of Millennial college students is expected to increase to 13.3 million, representing 75 percent of all college students (National Center for Education Statistics, 2005). These demographic projections illustrate the necessity of understanding this generation's values and beliefs in order to determine how to best educate its members.

The networked world that these students live in has dramatically influenced their view of the world and how they learn. Students in the Millennial Generation are characterized as multitaskers who are able to communicate equally well in person and online (Oblinger and Hawkins, 2005). This generation has grown up with video games and multiple types of technology. Gaming in all its aspects has many similarities with learning: learning experientially, learning interactively, and learning collaboratively (Sweeney, 2005).

Although many observations can be made about this generation, several merit listing due to the impact of their traits on higher education. Members of the Millennial Generation are intuitively visual communicators and can integrate the virtual and physical. This generation learns better through discovery than by being told what to do. They are able to shift their attention rapidly from one task to another and may choose not to pay attention. Last, they are able to respond quickly, and they expect rapid responses in return (Oblinger and Oblinger, 2005).

Learning style preferences of the Millennial Generation include hands-on experiential activities rather than lectures. These students are comfortable integrating the physical and the virtual. Their definition of technology differs from that of most faculty. If one defines technology as something that was created after a given generation was born, then the Web, computers, and networks are not considered technology to these students. The definition of technology from the Millennials' perspective is something that is new, novel, or customizable (Oblinger and Oblinger, 2005).

Technology Preferences of Millennials

Since students of this generation are tied to technology so much in their personal lives, it seems logical that Millennial students would prefer to use technology heavily in their education. However, this generation's comfort level with technology may not match their competency with technology used in an educational environment, as their underlying understanding of the technology may be shallow (Oblinger and Hawkins, 2005). "It is an almost instinctive assumption to believe that the Net Gen students will want to use IT [information technology] heavily in their education" (Oblinger and Oblinger, 2005, p. 2.10). Oblinger and Hawkins (2005) propose that Millennial learners do not think in terms of technology, because having technology available is a given. The activity enabled by the technology is more important than the technology itself to these students. The technology needs to take its place as an enabler of education rather than the focus. The students of this generation focus on what they want to learn, not on the technology that enables them to learn (Oblinger and Hawkins, 2005). Since members of the Millennial Generation spend so much time online, it is logical to expect that they would have a strong preference for Web-based instruction. "In theory, this generation should learn effectively through online course since they have been surrounded by computers all their lives" (Oblinger and Oblinger, 2005, p. 4.5).

The implication is that colleges and universities should not assume that more technology is necessarily better. Technology that enables certain types of activities is likely to be effective. For example, wireless technology enables learners to be mobile and constantly connected. Using technology to increase customization, convenience, and collaboration within academic environments is generally well-received by this generation; however, its integration into most courses or curricula is not as deep as into students' personal lives (Oblinger and Oblinger, 2005).

Definition of Web 2.0

Web 2.0 technologies are changing how we interact with each other and with our students. Web 2.0 is a multifaceted and somewhat ambiguous construct that can be described as participative and collaborative (Lindstrom, 2007). It refers to the newest generation of online applications that allow users to create and modify content. Web 2.0 represents the second generation of Internet services that is changing the form of online interaction and collaboration (O'Reilly, 2005). Terms such as "user-generated content," "software as service," "social networking," and the "read/write Web" describe this generation of the Web (Jones, 2008). Some of the most commonly cited tools are wikis and blogs, but hundreds of Web 2.0 tools have been developed over the past few years, allowing users to become active creators of Web content (Oliver, 2010). Although there is no precise definition, the term "Web 2.0" generally refers to the current generation of Web-based services and applications that allow users to collaborate, generate their own content, and share information online.

It was Dale Dougherty, the vice president of O'Reilly Media, who first used the term "Web 2.0" at a conference in 2004. This led to Tim O'Reilly's (2006) formal definition:

> Web 2.0 is the business revolution in the computer industry caused by the move to the internet as platform, and an attempt to understand the rules for success on that new platform. Chief among those rules is this: Build applications that harness network effects to get better the more people use them. This is what I've elsewhere called harnessing collective intelligence.

Web 2.0 tools allow users to create and share content online easily using blogs, social networks, and collaborative tools. In the previous Web 1.0 era, it was very difficult to publish information online, and knowledge of hyptertext markup language (HTML) was necessary in order to push content to the Web. Now the trend is user-driven content and collaboration implemented across multiple communities including education, consumers, and the business world. Multiuser virtual environments and ubiquitous computing allow users to move beyond the desktop interface to much more immersive environments that enhance learning. New learning styles will evolve based on mediated immersion and distributed learning communities (Oblinger and Oblinger, 2005).

A distinguishing characteristic of Web 2.0 tools is the ability to harness the collective intelligence and encourage teamwork, thus allowing users to share and collaborate. Each type of Web 2.0 tool accomplishes this task in a different way. Web 2.0 tools can be used to organize and manage information, enabling students to see patterns and relationships between pieces of information, and helping them to construct knowledge. Other tools create a space for collaboration, content development, and interaction, and encourage analysis and synthesis of information. Media sharing also is enabled by Web 2.0 technologies. When students create their own media, they are active participants in their own learning and create products that are shared and made available for others. Web 2.0 tools are classified into six categories in Table 1.1.

Popular Web 2.0 Tools

Blogs, or Web logs, are structured online journals that can be used for creative expression. Blogging allows users to solicit feedback on their blogposts; users also can post comments to other blogposts on their own blogs, linking back to the original blogpost. This trackback feature enables authors to keep track of who is linking to, and therefore referencing, their blogposts. The credibility of the blogger can be enhanced by the repeated linking to blogs created by that author. Blogs can be used as an instructional tool to enhance communication and reflection. Blogging may encourage students to become more analytical thinkers. Since others can critique

Table 1.1.   Classification of Social Software Tools

Category	Description	Examples
Communication tools	Web 2.0-enabled e-mail applications Web conferencing tools Instant messaging VoIP applications	Hotmail, Gmail Adobe Connect AIM Skype
Experience/Resource-sharing tools	Blogs, wikis Media sharing Social bookmarking	WordPress, Twitter Flickr, YouTube Delicious, Zotero
Social networking	Sites supporting social interaction through a dynamic set of networks	MySpace Facebook
Virtual worlds	Online community in the form of a computer-based simulated environment	Second Life Croquet
Online office tools	Applications enabling users to create, edit, and share information	Google Apps Microsoft Office Live
Mobile technologies	Digital audio players Smart phones	iPod, iTouch iPhone, Blackberry

Source: Kitsantas and Dabbagh (2010).

a blogpost, students need to be able to defend their positions based on critical thinking strategies (Oravec, 2002).

O'Reilly (2006), commenting on the power of blogging as a reflection of our thought processes, stated:

> If an essential part of Web 2.0 is harnessing collective intelligence, turning the web into a kind of global brain, the blogosphere is the equivalent of constant mental chatter in the forebrain, the voice we hear in all of our heads. It may not reflect the deep structure of the brain, which is often unconscious, but is instead the equivalent of conscious thought.

The significance of the blogosphere is thus recognized as having a powerful effect as a reflection of conscious thought and attention.

Wikis, other popular Web 2.0 tools, are collaborative Web sites that can be edited by anyone who has been given access. Wikis are a very flexible type of blog that supports collaborative and open editing and evolve as users add or edit material. Faculty may use wikis for collaborative projects in which students need to create, share, and manage content. Wikis also may be useful for sharing class notes in a course. Studies (Elgort, Smith, and Toland, 2008; Hazari, North, and Moreland, 2009) have shown that wikis can promote collaboration, encourage negotiation, and help make students comfortable with Web 2.0 technology tools. Wikis can be used for brainstorming, collaborative writing, and group discussions in order to promote student engagement (Kitsantas and Dabbagh, 2010).

Another popular tool is a podcast, a recorded audio or video file that is available over the Internet. This technology can be thought of as a merger between blogging and radio, an established broadcasting medium that people have listened to for generations. Podcasting is essentially radio programming that can be produced with a standard computer, microphone, free software, and a Web site for posting your programming. Podcasts can be listened to with any computer connected to the Internet and able to play standard MP3 audio files. Faculty may use podcasts to record and transmit various types of information, such as lectures, information on current events, or ancillary topics. Students may find podcasts inspiring and choose to create their own podcasts to showcase their learning or to share their reflections. Learners can add background music using programs such as Audacity or GarageBand and can upload their podcasts to iTunes to share with others (Richardson, 2009).

Nothing encapsulates the Web 2.0 concept more than social networking sites, which provide users the ability to connect, communicate, and share with others (O'Reilly, 2005). Social networking and user-created content are cited as new trends that will have a major impact on learning environments in higher education (EDUCAUSE Learning Initiative, 2010). A social networking site can be defined as a site that creates a community of individuals who share common interests. Examples are MySpace and Facebook. These sites are Web-based services that allow individuals to construct a public or semipublic profile within a bounded system, create a list of other users with whom they share a common interest, and navigate their list of connections as well as those made by others within the system (Boyd and Ellison, 2007). Social networking sites allow users to find others with similar interests, create personal reputations, collaborate, and share resources (Alexander, 2006).

Faculty can help students use social networking systems to create networks suited to their learning needs and interests. These types of networks can serve as support systems and learning environments that encourage collaboration and the sharing of resources. Students also can join existing groups on social networking sites that are focused on similar interests, courses, or professions (Kitsantas and Dabbagh, 2010).

Implications for Practice

The use of Web 2.0 tools in education builds on previous experiences with social networking that the Millennial Generation has experienced. The media convergence enabled by Web 2.0 technologies has created a new culture of "collective intelligence" in which individuals can build on each other's knowledge by forming "participatory communities" (Jenkins, 2006). Web 2.0 applications have the ability to change how educators interact with their students and with each other. Educators can utilize these tools to collaborate with students, colleagues, and other contacts.

The Internet is a constantly evolving infrastructure that now supports many Web 2.0 tools, including applications such as groupware for virtual collaboration, asynchronous threaded discussions, multiuser virtual environments, videoconferencing, and mobile devices. Research indicates that each of these media, when designed for education, fosters particular types of interactions that enable various learning styles (Oblinger and Oblinger, 2005).

Principles of good teaching, including participation and collaboration, are supported by Web 2.0 technologies. Individuals can build collectively on each other's knowledge by forming participative communities in which members contribute and pool collective knowledge. Jenkins (2006) compared the collective intelligence that occurs as a result of online participatory communities to the pedagogical process of scaffolding. This is the same process that occurs in the classroom when the instructor uses prior knowledge to provide support until students build confidence and master the material.

Kitsantas and Dabbagh (2010) defined three levels of social interactivity to support self-regulated learning that are enabled by Web 2.0 tools. At the first level of personal information management, students can use resource-sharing and online office tools to create a personal learning environment to manage course information on their own. At the second level, social interaction and collaboration, learners use communication and social networking tools to participate in learning communities focused on the course topics. In addition to performing a learning task at this level, students receive feedback from instructors and/or peers. At the third level, information aggregation, students use resource-sharing tools to aggregate information and reflect on their learning experience. This model allows the self-regulated learner to continue to adjust strategies for learning at the each of the three levels using Web 2.0 tools to optimize the learning experience.

Web 2.0: Looking Forward

Web 2.0 technologies promote open education and social learning. These technologies enable a powerful social and academic presence for educators. Having a social presence online and knowing how to leverage it help to promote personal and professional goals. Students can use the social networking power of Web 2.0 technologies to support their own learning. Institutions need to be able to leverage Web 2.0 tools in order to create and sustain learning communities that promote student success. Educators cannot afford to ignore the power of Web 2.0 technologies for student self-regulation, motivation, and learning.

The use of the Internet in education has become increasingly more common over the past decade, and technology has been used to facilitate learning both in the classroom and online. Distance learners have been able to communicate with their peers by using course management systems and Web 2.0 components that integrate with these systems. However, many factors impact learning outcomes besides technology. An educator using Web 2.0 tools needs to recognize that each tool is not an end unto itself. Many students may find Web 2.0 tools exciting; their use may engage such students more fully in the learning process. However, variables such as course content, pedagogy, and instructional technology influence learning as well as sound instructional practices (Mishra and Koehler, 2006). Research is needed to explore Web 2.0 technologies as they relate to learning outcomes in various disciplines. Additional studies are needed to determine what student learning styles of are best served by Web 2.0 technologies.

References

Alexander, B. "Web 2.0: A New Wave of Innovation for Teaching and Learning?" *Educause Review*, 2006, *41*(2), 32–44. Retrieved August 15, 2010, from http://net.educause.edu/ir/library/pdf/erm0621.pdf.

Boyd, D. M., and Ellison, N. B. "Social Network Sites: Definition, History, and Scholarship." *Journal of Computer-Mediated Communication*, 2007, *13*(1), article 11. Retrieved November 23, 2008, from jcmc.indiana.edu/vol13/issue1/boyd.ellison.html.

Brown, J. S. "Growing Up Digital: How the Web Changes Work, Education and the Ways People Learn." *Change*, 2000, *32*(2), 10–20.

Carlson, S. "The Net Generation Goes to College." *Chronicle of Higher Education*, 2005, *52*(7), A34.

Coomes, M., and DeBard, R. "A Generational Approach to Understanding Students," *New Directions for Student Services*, 2004, 106, Wiley Periodicals.

EDUCAUSE Learning Initiative. *The Seven Things You Need to Know about Privacy in Web 2.0 Learning Environments*. 2010. Retrieved September 23, 2010 from http://www.educause.edu/Resources/7ThingsYouShouldKnowAboutPriva/213085

Elgort, I., Smith, A. G,. and Toland, J. "Is wiki an effective platform for group course work?" *Australian Journal of Educational Technology*, 2008, 24(2), 195–210. Retrieved July 30, 2010, from http://www.ascilite.org.au/ajet/ajet24/elgort.html.

Hartman, J., Moskal, P., and Dziuban, C. "Preparing the Academy of Today for the Learner of Tomorrow." In D. G. Oblinger and J. L. Oblinger (eds.), *Educating the Net Generation* (pp. 6.1–6.15). 2005. EDUCAUSERetrieved May 14, 2010, from http://www.educause.edu/educatingthenetgen/.

Hazari, S., North, A., and Moreland, D. "Investigating Pedagogical Value of Wiki Technology." *Journal of Information Systems Education*, 2009, *20*(2), 187–198.

Jenkins, H. *Convergence Culture: Where Old and New Media Collide*. 2006, New York University Press.

Jones, B. (Ed.). *Interviews with 20 Web 2.0 Influences: Web 2.0 Heroes*. 2008, Indianapolis, IN: Wiley.

Kitsantas, A., and Dabbagh, N. *Learning to Learn with Integrative Learning Technologies (ILT): A Practical Guide for Academic Success*. Charlotte, N.C.: Information Age Publishing, 2010.

Lindstrom, P. "Securing Web 2.0 Technologies." Midvale, Utah: Burton Group *EDU-CAUSE Center for Applied Research*, 2007. Retrieved July 10, 2010, from http://www.educause.edu/ECAR/SecuringWeb20Technologies/158603.

Mishra, P., and Koehler, M. "Technological Pedagogical Content Knowledge: A Framework for Integrating Technology in Teacher Knowledge." *Teachers College Record*, 2006, *108*(6), 1017–1054.

National Center for Educational Statistics. *Digest of Educational Statistics, 2005*. Washington, D.C.: National Center for Educational Statistics, Retrieved November 11, 2006 from http://nces.ed.gov/pubsearch/pubsinfo.asp?pubid=2006030.

Oblinger, D. G., and Hawkins, B. L. "The Myth about Students." *Educause Review*, 2005, July/August.

Oblinger, D. G., and Oblinger, J. L. (2005). *Educating the Net Generation*, Boulder, Colo.: Educause. http://www.educause.edu/educatingthenetgen.

Oliver, K. "Integrating Web 2.0 Across the Curriculum." *TechTrends*, March, 2010, *54*(2), 50–60.

Oravec, J. "Bookmarking the World: Weblog Applications in Education." *Journal of Adolescent and Adult Literacy*, 2002, 45(7), 616–621.

O'Reilly, T. "What Is Web 2.0? Design Patterns and Business Models for the Next Generation of Software." 2005. Retrieved May 14, 2010, from http://oreilly.com/web2/archive/what-is-web-20.html.

O'Reilly, T. "Web. 2.0 Compact Definition: Trying Again." O'Reilly Radar, December 2006. Retrieved June 29, 2010, from http://radar.oreilly.com/2006/12/web-20-compact-definition-tryi.html.

Prensky, M. "Digital Natives, Digital Immigrants." October 2001. Retrieved July 12, 2010, from http://www.marcprensky.com/writing.

Richardson, W. *Blogs, Wikis, Podcasts, and Other Power Web Tools for Classrooms* (2nd ed.) Thousand Oaks, Calif.: Corwin Press, 2009.

Skiba, D. and Barton, A. "Adapting Your Teaching to Accommodate the Net Generation of Learners." *Online Journal of Issues in Nursing*, 2006, 11(2), 15. Retrieved February 15, 2008, from: http://www.nursingworld.org/ojin/topic30/tpc30_4.htm.

Sweeney, R. "Colloquy." *Chronicle of Higher Education*, October 5, 2005, p. A15.

Tapscott, D. *Growing Up Digital: The Rise of the Net Generation*. New York: McGraw-Hill, 1998.

SUSANNE K. BAJT, Ed.D., is a graduate of the department of Human Resource Education at the University of Illinois at Urbana-Champaign and is a professor of Computer Information Systems at William Rainey Harper College in Palatine, IL.

NEW DIRECTIONS FOR COMMUNITY COLLEGES • DOI: 10.1002/cc

6

As this and previous editions of New Directions for Community Colleges *have argued, digital skills are necessary. Our future economy will be based on them, but there is no consensus on which skills to teach. Many talk about Web 2.0 skills, familiarity with software, and critical thinking skills, yet few mention the potential of video games in education. This chapter examines the potential for using video games at the community college level, possible arguments against it, and necessary support from administration, information technology departments, and libraries to make the most of this digital technology.*

Andragogy, Organization, and Implementation Concerns for Gaming as an Instructional Tool in the Community College

Vance S. Martin

Research

Two recent studies provide a sense of the ubiquity of video games. A recent PEW research study found that 99 percent of boys and 94 percent of girls age twelve to seventeen play video games. Fifty percent of these students played a game the previous day (Lenhart and others, 2008). This is and will be a part of the traditional community college population. However, this is not to exclude returning students, since the average age of video game players is thirty-five, with 25 percent of Americans over fifty playing video games (Entertainment Software Association, n.d.).

These studies are interesting but may not immediately overcome teachers' and administrators' concerns regarding integrating games into instruction.

NEW DIRECTIONS FOR COMMUNITY COLLEGES, no. 154, Summer 2011 © 2011 Wiley Periodicals, Inc.
Published online in Wiley Online Library (wileyonlinelibrary.com) • DOI: 10.1002/cc.447

However, work within the field of video games and education that discusses increased engagement of students may make some rethink this position. Students already familiar with the medium of video games are able to make connections more readily between games and courses in which they are utilized. These connections are more problematic in traditional classes, when students unfamiliar with academic writing, political systems, ancient history, or child development are asked to receive knowledge passively through instruction. In their free time students are actively experiencing and creating knowledge with video games and other online applications. Active learning through video games fills a hole in the traditional passive educational model. Instructors who can make the connection between their content knowledge and games offer a powerful interaction and interrelation. This is related to the idea of andragogy, or adult learning strategies, which attempts to engage adult learners with the structure of learning experience.

Some background in the literature may help those still questioning the idea of using video games in a classroom. One of the seminal works in education and video games is by James Gee (2003). His work integrates the constructivist works of Bakhtin, Bordieu, and Vygotsky, looking at how players construct knowledge while playing video games. Games allow players to begin slowly, at a lower level, and over time increase their skills and knowledge as they become experts at a game. As Kurt Squire (2010) has recently discussed, there is a learning scale in video game use. As players progress from "newbs," or neophytes, to intermediate and expert players, a change occurs. As a player becomes expert, she wants to tinker with the game and become a community leader within the online game. Some studies also link this level of play to increased activism. It is at this level of expertise that the cross between disciplinary learning and gaming can occur.

Possibilities

Some examples may illustrate what Gee and Squire are talking about. Dona Cady (2010), at Middlesex Community College in Bedford, Massachusetts, has integrated online games into her humanities courses. In one of these courses, she had her students sign up for a ten-day free trial of *World of Warcraft*. This is an online immersive environment with over 11 million players worldwide. The students played the game with classmates for ten days and kept a journal of their travels and experiences. They then revised and submitted their journals for their writing assignments. Some students wrote as if they were explorers, some as battlefield journalists, and some as anthropologists "going native" as their characters within the social world of the game. For an assignment for which students had traditionally balked at writing ten to twelve pages, the average submission for this assignment was over seventy pages.

NEW DIRECTIONS FOR COMMUNITY COLLEGES • DOI: 10.1002/cc

One need not integrate actual video games into a class; in some cases video game–like ideas will work. Roger Travis (Travis and Young, 2010) at the University of Connecticut operates his courses as text-based games. His classics courses then operate as role-playing video games. In a role-playing game players earn experience points for going on a quest or fighting a dragon, and with enough experience points they earn a level. In this class students earn experience points for doing assignments, and they gain levels based on total experience points. In essence, Travis simply has changed assignment points to experience and grades to levels, but the cumulative effect to the grades and the reception by students has been amazing. Students used to game mechanics put more effort in the class to attain a higher level than they felt they would have with simply a grading scale. These ideas also have been used successfully at the University of Edinburgh's School of Medicine (Begg, Dewhurst, and Macleod, 2005).

The author has used the video game *Civilization* in his own online and on-campus history instruction for several years. This game is an historical strategy game that allows players to experience history as different nations. One student at the intermediate level wrote: "The video game allows history to become a more hands-on class; which is something I did not think history ever had a chance at becoming." Another student, who had advanced to mastery level and began to tinker with the game, felt that with the ability to replay scenarios he could fail and try again, truly learning and testing out his own ideas. Several international students also felt the game was a way to gain a sense for the material without relying on a specific language (Martin, 2008). These findings tie in with some ongoing work of Rich Halverson, who is using games to teach medical students. The games that he is helping to develop teach the larger themes and skills necessary for medical students and introduce technical jargon after basic ideas have been conveyed and students have a context for them (Halverson, Bauman, Wolfenstein, Millar, and Patterson, 2010). Such teaching could be referred to as just-in-time teaching.

Potential Arguments

Engagement and active learning increase with these games, yet most teachers are not using them. There must be a reason for this reluctance and a way to overcome it. Next we examine some of the potential reasons and counterarguments. Perhaps through examination and explanation, the reluctance may decrease. The main issues can be broken down into themes: preconceived notions, time, money, bandwidth, and security.

Preconceived Notions. To most people, video games are simply recreational. Depending on age, some people may envision *Pong*, *Space Invaders*, *Super Mario Brothers*, or *Grand Theft Auto*, but most people would categorize them with fun, not homework. Years of schooling have shown instructors and administrators that hard work, studying texts, and doing homework are the way to understand course material and thereby succeed. Video game integration potentially could make an instructor or the discipline appear less rigorous. However, some large universities such as the University of Wisconsin, Carnegie Mellon, Stanford, the University of Southern California, and Indiana University have large programs examining video games in education. Their focus and expenditure of time and money show that there is interest and value in integrating videogames and education. Their graduates are securing jobs in academia, video game design, and workforce education, making future integration of games in education easier.

Time. Related to the concern over schoolwork and fun is the problem of time. Every teacher is busy with course preparation, grading, office hours, and committee work, without including family or other responsibilities. Teachers have little time in their schedule to play a video game just to see if it might be useful for their courses. But in order to integrate a game, they must play it to see if it is useful. They may even become frustrated because the first game they picked was not applicable, so they have to try another one. They also may test a game in a class and it may not succeed the first time. However, would any faculty member suggest that their schedule is too busy for the effort of preparing a new class or using a new textbook? In order to instruct better, teachers need to reflect on their practice and what works, integrating new knowledge into their instruction. This is true with video games as well as research.

Money. Another concern with implementation of video games is cost. This concern arises on various levels. Some researchers claim that the best games are those specifically developed for a discipline, games termed "epistemic" (Shafer, 2005). Developing games can be expensive, but doing so for one course alone would be almost cost prohibitive. Although costs have decreased, the minimum expenditure would be $100,000. Mobile games (m-games) for mobile devices are cheaper to develop yet still can cost tens of thousands of dollars. Currently, only large universities and governments can afford to develop epistemic games, although that may change as prices and technological hurdles decrease ("80Days—Around an Inspiring Virtual Learning World in Eighty Days.").

A second option is using commercially available games. These games cost around $50 apiece and can be played on computers or platforms such as the Wii or Xbox. However, the question still remains: Who pays for the games, the school or the instructor? If the decision is made to make a game part of the curriculum, who should pay, the school or the student? These are tough questions in our current economy and will need to be discussed by the faculty and administration. Depending on how integral the game is to a course, it may be possible to require students to buy it. They purchase textbooks that can cost hundreds of dollars. They are more willing to purchase a game than textbooks. This method can sidestep some potential copyright concerns: If students own the game, they have the right to play it. It is possible to sell the game and the rights would transfer, similar to textbook buybacks. A school could show its support for games by having the library acquire copies, as the University of Illinois has done. This could be useful for prospective instructors as well as students. A library with a growing video game collection may be the way to allow instructors to test games prior to purchase. This method also will show administrative support for video game instruction.

Some instructors have taken different approaches to integrating video games into their classes and have wrestled with the issue of cost. For example, Cady had her students take advantage of free trial periods. Travis simply integrated video game ideas into his instruction, which cost the students nothing. The author had students purchase the game. Another option is to use one of the increasing number of free games on Facebook and online, such as *Mafia Wars* on Facebook or *Runes of Magic*. Wikipedia lists over one hundred of these free massively multiplayer onlines (MMOs).

Bandwidth.   Information technology departments are perennially concerned with bandwidth problems. They may be concerned about the extra load even without including online video games. To counter these concerns, Peggy Sheehy and Lucas Gillispie recently have had students in New York and North Carolina collectively play *World of Warcraft* (Gillispie, Sheehy, and Lawson, 2010). Initially they were concerned that there might be bandwidth problems. However, once they began, the authors found that opening Gmail takes more bandwidth than playing *World of Warcraft*. There will always be bandwidth concerns regarding faculty listening to Internet radio in their office and/or watching *Family Guy* on Hulu. Games, however, are optimized for performance to sell to larger audiences. Information technology departments that are still are concerned could restrict these games to off-peak times for a testing period.

Security.   A final concern some may have is that of security. Will these games open the school to extra viruses? Will students unknowingly give out too much information and have their identities stolen? If using Facebook games, could personal information be used against people? These are all valid concerns, which the instructors, the administration, and the information technology departments should think about and discuss. There will be less concern with these issues if instructors use games played only against computers. More of these problems will arise with online, interactive games. Instructors should think about foreseeable risks and be ready to act when unforeseen events occur. With many commercial games, the companies that produce them have a vested interest in keeping their players/customers safe. Granted, concerns over the definition of safe may vary, as seen recently with Facebook security settings. A potential solution could be taken from Gillispie, Sheehy, and Lawson (2010) who, in a K–12 setting, controlled usernames and passwords and set parental controls on the accounts to limit student play to allowed times. Penn State developed a two-tier system where students used their campus passwords on a sign-in computer, which would physically unlock a case on another computer on which they could then sign in to the actual games. Penn State also had to convince the central information technology department to allow more frequent updates of operating systems and games themselves, because conservative departments often want to wait to see if an update is stable (Bixler, 2010).

Example from Practice

An example of my own travails may help give readers an idea of the process of game integration. In early 2007, my department chair approved the possibility of integrating *Civilization* into a history class. She added a Spring 2008 history section to the schedule, specifying that students would have to buy the game. Several students showed interest by e-mail, but the class did not have enough students to constitute a full section and was canceled. Instead, I was assigned an online section and decided to offer the game as a final project option. The department chair purchased several copies of the game and coordinated with the information technology department to install the games and updates in the computer lab. However, the game disks had to be in the drive for the game to operate. This caused a concern over theft or loss, which meant the game could be played in the lab only when the lab monitor was there. Because of this, students mainly played online from home, with each other. Since then the department chair has been supportive, listing a specific section of the class with the video game every summer, which always fills. I've continued to use games in online and on-campus courses.

There have been problems on the student and faculty sides with this implementation. Some students, often those concerned with their grades, do not feel that a video game will add any value to their education. Over several semesters of use, this concern has disappeared. Colleagues are supportive but have found difficulty integrating the game into their own classes. Some teachers have allowed the author to oversee their students playing the game. However, students seem hesitant to ask for help from someone other than their instructor. Because of this, the instructors have seen the need to play the games themselves and have been testing it. Teachers need to know why they are using a game and be able to explain the reason to students. Teachers are also the first line of troubleshooting and answering technical questions for students. They need to know how to solve potential technological problems that could occur with a game. Most students are computer savvy, so these problems are easily solved when their technological skills are nudged by a helpful instructor with some experience.

The Future

It is important for the faculty and administration to stay up to date with research in the field of technology applications to education, and to engage their students in a medium in which they are familiar. Beyond this, administrators need to reach out to department chairs to encourage instructors to participate if they want to engage students and teach twenty-first-century skills. Doing this will require instructors to test games on their own to see how a game may be applicable to their discipline. To facilitate this, the administration will need to work with the library, the information technology department, department chairs, and teachers. Teachers may need to use school computers to test games. They may need the library to incur the cost of a game in order to test it. Although the game *The Sims 3* may work poorly for an economics instructor, it may work marvelously for a sociology instructor. After several semesters of support, the initial instructors may find that a certain game does not work for them, but actually may connect with other instructors for whom it might work. This will help change faculty perceptions of games. Again, however, without continued support from the administration, instructors will see little need for this interaction. Without personal support from the department chair or the information technology department, the author's use of video games may never have come to fruition.

Administrative support is key in several areas for encouraging instructors to use games for education. This support can be shown through department heads, information technology departments, or library acquisitions. In some venues, it also may be shown in creating a gaming commons, as has been done at Penn State (Bixler, 2010). Penn State has a lab with powerful computers, gaming platforms, and many games. The lab develops games for classes and helps link educators with potentially useful games. A lab like Penn State's is expensive, but it could be a part of a school's long-term plan or something for grant writers to consider.

Although there are obstacles to overcome, there are also benefits to the use of a video game in the classroom. Instructors may have problems in the first semester implementing a video game in their instruction, but they will see more engagement from students in the project than they have in the past. That engagement and interest in the discipline will encourage instructors to keep up with the project and perhaps even look for other ways to integrate games. The author continually looks for ways to integrate games for himself and colleagues.

The community college is best poised among educational institutions for integration of games. Unlike elementary and secondary schools, which must teach to nationalized tests and have larger bureaucracies, community colleges can focus on content and understanding of knowledge. They can also allow individual instructors more freedom. And unlike K–12 schools and larger colleges and universities with larger bureaucracies, community colleges can be more streamlined in their introduction of games. Games can be introduced into courses with large offerings or online courses. They can be tested with one teacher and expanded at a later date.

All games have educational potential; however, it is through the vision of instructors that active learning can occur. These instructors need to believe in the value of the game as a teaching tool; otherwise, students will not see the value and will find its use inauthentic. Most teachers will not get to this point, though, if they do not see the support from various groups on campus: department chairs, teaching centers, information technology departments, libraries, and administration. Right now faculty members on campuses across the nation play video games and would be willing to bring them into the classroom as a test group. However, their own educational background within their field does not support this practice; in addition, they know what people think about games. What they need is support. This support could be a kindly recommendation from a department chair, paid incentives for a small test group of instructors, or simply campus-wide recognition. This support will create engaged students with increased digital skills.

References

"80Days—Around an Inspiring Virtual Learning World in Eighty Days." (n.d.). Retrieved October 15, 2009, from http://www.eightydays.eu/.

Begg, M., Dewhurst, D., and Macleod, H. "Game-Informed Learning: Applying Computer Game Processes to Higher Education. *Innovate: Journal of Online Education*, 2005, *1*(6). Retrieved October 1, 2010, from http://innovateonline.info/index.php?view=article&id=176&action=synopsis.

Bixler, B. "Twenty Billion Reasons to Build an Educational Gaming Initiative in Higher Education." Paper presented at the Games+Learning+Society 6.0 in Madison, Wisconsin, 2010.

Entertainment Software Association. (n.d.). "Industry Facts." Retrieved October 1, 2010, from http://www.theesa.com/facts/index.asp.

Gee, J. P. *What Video Games Have to Teach Us about Learning and Literacy.* New York: Palgrave Macmillan, 2003.

Gillispie, L., Sheehy, P., and Lawson, C. "Learning with the Lich King: Education in *World of Warcraft.*" Paper presented at the Games+Learning+Society 6.0 in Madison, Wisconsin, 2010.

Halverson, R., Bauman, E., Wolfenstein, M., Millar, S., and Patterson, N. "Progression: Advancing the Development and Adoption of Games for Learning." Paper presented at the Games+Learning+Society 6.0 in Madison, Wisconsin, 2010.

Lenhart, A., Kahne, J., Middaugh, E., Macgill, A.R., Evans, C., and Vitak, J. "Teens, Video Games, and Civics." Pew Internet and American Life Project. 2008. Retrieved September 29, 2008, from http://www.pewinternet.org/Reports/2008/Teens-Video-Games-and-Civics.aspx.

Martin, V. S. "Online Video Games in an Online History Class." Paper presented at the Second IEEE International Conference on Digital Game and Intelligent Toy Enhanced Learning DIGITEL in Banff, Alberta, Canada, 2008.

Shafer, D. W. Epistemic Games. *Innovate: Journal of Online Ed*, 2005, *1*(6). Retrieved October 1, 2010, from http://innovateonline.info/index.php?view=article&id=79&action=synopsis.

NEW DIRECTIONS FOR COMMUNITY COLLEGES • DOI: 10.1002/cc

Squire, K. *Video Games and Education*. Unpublished manuscript, Madison, Wisc., 2010.
Travis, R. and Young, M. "Operation KTHMA—Reign of the Demiurge: Game Worlds, Greek History, the Classics, and Situated Learning." Paper presented at the Games+Learning+Society 6.0 in Madison, Wisconsin, 2010.

VANCE S. MARTIN, PhD., has worked as an instructor with the Community College Teaching and Learning program at the University of Illinois and teaches history at Parkland College in Champaign, IL.

7

Discussion of leadership functions and practices in the realm of instructional technology in community colleges cannot be limited to the administrative side. Faculty members and faculties as collective bodies have influenced or attempted to influence the use of instructional technology and can claim professionally to have the right to participate heavily in decision making.

Faculty Leadership and Instructional Technologies: Who Decides?

Bob Barber

The use of personal computer (PC) technology in community college learning environments and instructional processes has generated controversy and conflict since its inception. Some faculty members reacted negatively from the start. Others, in many disciplines beyond computer science, were intrigued by the new capabilities of PCs but found institutions reluctant to release control over what had been a purely administrative use of centralized mainframe computers. During the 1990s, faculty and other academic leaders and staff sought to apply the PC in a variety of ways, mostly learning informally by trial and error (Barber, 2010; de los Santos, Jr., and Story, 2001). The 1990s were also the time when the emergence of networks signaled a shift from using computers as desktop tools to using them as communication tools and as gateways to "content" (Diaz and Cheslock, 2006, p. 63). This shift made possible what is now known as distributed learning (where instructors and students are separated to some degree over time and location), which is having a major impact on faculty responsibilities, faculty work, and faculty culture.

This chapter draws on research and practitioner literature on faculty and the organizational aspects of technology and distributed learning to address the extent to which faculty in community colleges have a role in decision making regarding technology. In particular, the chapter aims to answer three questions:

New Directions for Community Colleges, no. 154, Summer 2011 © 2011 Wiley Periodicals, Inc.
Published online in Wiley Online Library (wileyonlinelibrary.com) • DOI: 10.1002/cc.448

1. How is instructional technology incorporated or not incorporated into shared governance systems and into collective bargaining agreements, where they exist?
2. How are issues of curriculum development and content decided with regard to the use of instructional technology?
3. How can faculty participate proactively and provide leadership in the use of technology in learning environments and instructional processes?

Theoretical Framework

Decision making regarding technology in instruction is driven by organizational culture as well as technical options. Community college faculty and administrators and support staff determine the kind of organizational culture in practice in institutions and are in the best position to address the issues raised by the dramatic impact of information technology on every aspect of their work and working lives. As in other areas, decision making regarding technology is driven by the governance structures, processes, and principles of a community college. Participants (faculty, administrators, support staff) have varying interests and thus various viewpoints on how, when, and why to use technology in the instructional program.

Organizational culture has tremendous impact on how technology will be used. March and Olsen (1995, p. 29) point out that "interests are shaped by institutional arrangements. Institutions also shape the definition of alternatives and influence the perception and construction of the reality within which action takes place. Institutional capabilities and structures affect the flow of information, the kinds of searches undertaken, and the interpretations made of the results."

Levin (2001) suggests that, at the extreme, community colleges have become like several institutions within one, "multi-institutions" that have several internal structures oriented toward different elements of their external environment. For example, a college might have one relationship with a nearby university for transfer articulation; another set of relationships with private sector employers who want training for their employees; another set of "virtual" relationships with a subset of students and with other institutions sharing courses and programs, perhaps online; and other relationships with professional associations that set standards for a variety of professional training. In this sense, community colleges are prototypical of the emerging organizational typology, called "adhocracy" by Mintzberg (1983). These types of organizations are characterized by the existence of multiple subsystems with varying goals and flexible boundaries, held together by an overall mission along with, increasingly, information technology. No longer are community colleges so narrowly typical of the traditional bureaucracy, as portrayed by Birnbaum (1988).

Power in community colleges also can be viewed using Mintzberg's typology of "internal systems of influence": the systems of Authority,

New Directions for Community Colleges • DOI: 10.1002/cc

Ideology, Expertise, and Politics. The extent to which the systems are in balance, or one system is in ascendancy, at any given time will determine the configuration of power and thus decision-making processes (Mintzberg, 1983). Community colleges experience conflict among these systems, particularly because the system of Authority derives from the hierarchical high school model yet the faculty is steeped in the systems of Ideology and Expertise. With multiple missions, institutional interests, and internal systems as well as external pressures, a wide range of decisions will be impacted by the interplay of these systems. Decisions about the use of information technology have particular impact in this environment, because technology is now so critical in record keeping, in core communications capability, and in the learning environment. In this chapter, the interrelated issues of organizational culture and systems of power will be brought to bear on decision making about instructional technology.

External Pressures

Accompanying this development is a set of externally driven influences on the culture of community colleges, where increases in external complexity cause increased internal complexity both for the organization and for its members (Scott, 1992). Organizations modify their goals and ways of operating in response to pressures from their external environment, although they can contribute to the creation of that environment as well. When such external factors impact institutions of higher education, they interact with a particular set of organizational characteristics (Kezar, 2001), although with at least one increasingly important exception. Kezar discusses the "relative independence" of higher education institutions from their environment. Although once this may have been true, community colleges in the late twentieth century became increasingly buffeted by global social, political, and technological forces (Levin, 2001).

Several external pressures on colleges must be noted in the realm of computer technology. By the 2000s, a high degree of standardization and routinization was emerging in the use of technology in instruction in community colleges. PC hardware and software industries consolidated quickly through the 1980s and 1990s. No community college could withstand, even if it wanted to, the standardization of desktop software to the Microsoft Office suite and the elimination of alternatives such as WordPerfect, nor the institutional marginalization of the Macintosh to a few niches.

The "user interface" for Internet-based instructional design also was moved rapidly from faculty-generated, self-made hypertext markup language (HTML) Web pages to standardized course management systems such as Blackboard, WebCT, and the open-source Moodle. According to the 2009 Campus Computing Survey, the percentage of community colleges using course management systems/learning management systems rose from slightly over 10 percent in 2000 to nearly 50 percent in 2009 (Green,

New Directions for Community Colleges • DOI: 10.1002/cc

2009). These systems present a standardized format for posting materials, having discussion forums or two-way e-mail conversations, and generally operating the infrastructure of a class.

In the world of course management software, debate is emerging as to whether the commercial course management systems will flounder in the face of open-source tools, which are cheaper and allow greater local modification of interfaces and capabilities (Gonick, 2009; Green, 2009).

Impacts on Faculty Culture

Garza Mitchell (2009) studied a successful instance in which faculty took advantage of new technological capabilities to change their outlook and practice of teaching; in other words, there was change in the organizational culture. Distance learning in its interactive form, with learning independent of time and place, required a cultural rethinking by faculty. Even as faculty members modify their approaches, however, the pedagogical rationale for use of technology in instruction remains heavily contested, and its outcomes or even measurability are uncertain (Garza Mitchell, 2010). Underlying issues regarding the nature of faculty work and the role of faculty in institutional decision-making have emerged. Dickson (1999) applies Scott's (1992) work to point out that the increasing technical complexity of the external environment of community colleges is leading to increased internal structural complexity and increased complexity on the part of the "performers" (faculty and, in a somewhat different way, administrative and support staff).

Impact on the organizational structure can be found in the various ways colleges administer and support technology, not just in administrative tasks but also in instructional processes and faculty training, and in the changes wrought by the increasing use of part-time instructors. Faculty culture is being impacted by the institutional expectation that instructional patterns will change and computer technology will be used. Full-time faculty members are becoming managers in the framework of designing curriculum and then handing it off to part-timers to teach. Smith and Rhoades (2006) and Hanson (2008) provide detailed descriptions of an emerging course design model of this type; they argue that it should alarm faculty and all those concerned with the academic enterprise in community colleges.

Hanson (2008) describes an instructional design system developed for the technical colleges of Wisconsin and later marketed more widely. He refers to this system as a form of Taylorism: The student passes through a linear set of preordained objectives, making the process an expression of industrial-era management strategy. "The . . . development process calls on instructors to design courses into the software by answering questions of WHAT students are to learn, WHEN, and HOW—but nothing about WHY" (Hanson, 2008, p. 73).

NEW DIRECTIONS FOR COMMUNITY COLLEGES • DOI: 10.1002/cc

Smith and Rhoades (2006) provide a comprehensive description of three modes of course development, one of which, the "virtual assembly line," they describe as the technology-driven model that seems highly appealing to at least some administrators. They studied three high-enrollment courses as developed and taught at three different colleges in a community college district: introductory English, introductory psychology, and introductory computer applications. One college used the course development model Smith and Rhoades label "craft"—a single professor does all the work and the course is idiosyncratic in that sense. Work is highly "bundled" in the traditional faculty sense. The second college had a "collegial" model—a team works on the courses but divides labor by skills and interests, and all have input into all facets if they want. Each team member can do things slightly differently from the others if they want to. There is a "high degree of bundling." The third college has what is labeled the "virtual assembly line"—the creation and teaching of a course is unbundled. This college has 30 full-time faculty members and 955 adjunct instructors, of whom 538 are distance instructors. In this college, eight aspects of course creation are separated from each other (unbundled) and assigned to different personnel, some faculty, some not. Those who are technology specialists report to a managerial structure that is not academically led. Not all the "content experts" are faculty; some may be "outside experts." Different experts may be used for creating lessons, for making quizzes, and for designing the final exam.

Smith and Rhoades (2006) conclude that the craft and collegial control models offer the possibility of adapting to the new world of instructional technology while allowing professors to exercise central responsibility for ensuring that teaching and learning processes prioritize broader educational purposes over narrower ones of maximizing efficiencies. They argue that "it is up to professors . . . in their academic departments and colleges, and in their collective bargaining units, to shape the model by which instructional technologies will be used and how instructional delivery will be organized" (pp. 109–110).

Who Is Deciding?

These trends bring up the question of governance. Amey and VanDerLinden (2003) conclude that attention must be paid to deciding who controls and participates in establishing the policy agenda and infrastructure associated with information and instructional technology. It is not surprising that there will be variation in views on technology issues because different people and units are impacted differently. Major technology transitions are organizational transitions. A "culture of campus-wide involvement" is needed.

But are faculty members positioned and able to meet this challenge? Faculty members and faculty as collective bodies have influenced or attempted to influence the use of instructional technology as issues of learning effectiveness, academic freedom, workload, and faculty control of the curriculum and the future faculty workforce, and their own intellectual property. Yet the evidence suggests that they are not substantially involved in technology decision-making via governance or collective bargaining.

• Major changes are being wrought in faculty work without their direct participation in the decisions, raising questions regarding how instructional technology is incorporated into shared governance systems and collective bargaining agreements.

Community colleges have long been known for their organizational roots in high schools with their strong-principal system and lack of faculty voice. There is not a tradition of shared governance. Nevertheless, community college leaders have realized that they need to find new approaches to leadership, both participatory and pluralistic (Kezar, 1998). As Levin, Kater, and Wagoner (2006) have noted, community colleges are increasingly orienting themselves toward an organizational mission and structure that is in line with the "new economy" or the "information economy." They are playing an economic role by emphasizing job skills, adopting managerialism as the leadership philosophy, and relegating faculty to the sidelines in decision making except insofar as participation in governance is bargained for increased faculty productivity. In the face of decreased state support, community colleges have become more entrepreneurial, which includes shifting even further toward part-time faculty. Some of the changes in orientation toward economic competition are structural and involve labor alterations, including substantial increases in the use of instructional technology. In this assessment, instructional technology has less to do with learning and more to do with achieving or hoping to achieve efficiencies of scale that can decrease costs and increase revenues (Diaz and Cheslock, 2006).

Rhoades and Maitland (2004) point out that the degree to which faculty are proactive in ensuring participation in technology-related decisions has long-range implications. "Technology is changing the way colleges organize and deliver instruction for distance education and on campus. These changes affect the workload of current faculty and the future structure of the professional workforce" (p. 75). The problem is that bargaining often addresses the workload of current faculty more than the future configuration of the whole workforce.

Maitland, Rhoades, and Smith (2009) report that the majority of faculty union contracts in the large National Education Association Higher Education Contract Analysis System (HECAS) "still fail to recognize the impact of distance learning on individual faculty members and on the collective faculty workforce" (p. 82). But important exceptions specify varying degrees of faculty control over distance education, although fewer contracts address on-campus, classroom-based instructional technology. They urge faculty to attempt to regulate on-campus as well as online technology and to work with faculty senates to ensure sound academic policies and the quality of the instructional program.

Finally, no data have been found that specifically study technology decision making in governance systems of community colleges outside of collective bargaining. Some chief information officers have advisory committees to get stakeholder input on decisions and/or work with the executive leadership team to set priorities (Armstrong, Simer, and Spaniol, 2011).

• How are issues of curriculum development and content decided with regard to the use instructional technology?

A large part of the work of community college faculty involves designing effective learning environments and curriculum. It is their expert knowledge of learning frameworks and models that gives faculty members their professional authority to design learning environments for students. Mintzberg (1983) describes this type of expertise as a Professional Bureaucracy and the systems of authority that are associated with it as the systems of Ideology and Expertise. The culture of faculty as professional experts has been built around these beliefs, but the degree to which they translate into effective authority in community colleges is mixed. In addition to having inherited the strong-principal, weak-faculty high school system, community college faculty members have been criticized for being disconnected from their disciplines and mired in a practitioner culture.

In the framework of technology, this question can be examined at the levels of (a) course content, (b) course design, and (c) modes of interaction (sometimes called "delivery method"). In fact, separating these aspects is not easy. The capabilities and constraints raised by information technologies make separation even more difficult. Course content is circumscribed by a variety of factors that have little to do with computers *per se*—overall learning goals, a discrete portion of a body of knowledge, and a particular set of experiences. But those factors cannot be sorted out without addressing course design (who does what—instructor with students, or students with other students—when, and how?). Of course the question of "how" brings the problem to modes of interaction. And the modes of interaction in community college classes have changed dramatically because of information technologies.

Some colleges have specific clauses in their faculty contracts which ensure that distance courses are subject to the same approval process as on-campus courses; such clauses establish a benchmark equivalency. However, the trend toward the use of course management systems like Blackboard or open-source equivalents represents a new turn in course development and presentation. This is an entirely new method of interaction between instructors and students. Who is making the decisions about their use? Rhoades and Maitland (2004) ask whether faculty must use the commercial course management programs.

> These technologies can help faculty coordinate their curricular objectives and lessons. But these platforms may also: (a) standardize instruction and instructors; (b) advance a competency-based model of education in which these tools are explicitly embedded; and (c) ensure the increased involvement of other professionals and paraprofessionals who chose the platforms, maintain these technologies, train and support faculty, and develop technology-intensive materials (p. 76).

Rhoades and Maitland suggest that faculty are impacted significantly by the introduction of course management systems, but there is no mention of faculty bargaining over the issue.

Clash of Cultures?

Faculty are expressing their views about the role of technology in instruction in a variety of ways, some formal, some less so. Villanti (2003) highlights the faculty members who resisted the rush to online courses, not out of fear of technology but for pedagogical reasons. A new type of faculty-created course quickly emerged, now called "hybrid," in which some aspects of the course activities take place in a classroom and some online. Faculty members at some colleges have negotiated contract language regarding the process of introducing and delivering technology-based classes. Increasing numbers of colleges are adopting open-source course management software to allow greater customization and reduce dependence on commercial products. Faculty as teachers and as researchers are pointing toward and acting on key pedagogical issues, such as the importance of place in a virtual world (Dolce and Morales-Vasquez, 2003), the benefits of the classroom experience (Shpancer, 2004), and the cultural biases built into computer-based instruction that may favor students from individualistic cultures but penalize those from more collaborative cultures (Smith and Ayers, 2006).

But community college faculty members are also in a contradictory position. While seeing their profession being transformed by the ways in which technology is being introduced, they are also the beneficiaries of technology (Diaz and Cheslock, 2006; Levin, Kater, and Wagoner, 2006). Technology makes it possible to work more efficiently in some ways, but also adds work and extends work hours. To a large extent, faculty members are not collectively resisting, although no doubt many individual faculty members work to ensure that they can control as much of the technology within their reach as possible.

When I worked as a community college computer literacy and user support instructor, I participated in the heady days of the 1990s when experimentation and sharing among faculty were the order of the day. I saw technology become one of the most sharply debated topics between faculty and administration at the bargaining table and in governance committees. I joined in efforts to find ways of applying technology in different ways in different disciplines but also saw how the capability could have the effect of changing how faculty and students work together in the learning environment. I also experienced the closing in of the commons as the world of hardware and software became highly standardized and the idea of doing it yourself was declared impractical. I helped design innovative ways of combining technology skills with faculty teaching skills and also led institutional training in highly standardized systems. The principal lesson I learned from all of this is how critical variety is to learning environments and organizational cultures (Barber, 2010).

Underlying the phenomena discussed in this chapter is the central role that communications and communications capability plays in human life and in educational environments (Dickson, 1999). Technological developments that intensify communications can be counted on to continue to disrupt the practices of learning-oriented institutions like community colleges. New devices and interfaces are affecting the communication capabilities and expectations of students. The emergence of personal communications devices and social networking technology is bringing new dimensions of communication and flexibility into the learning environment. This fact has implications not only for student learning and administrative requirements but also for the design and carrying out of faculty work.

Who decides whether using this or any technology leads to more effective learning and learning environments for students? This question has local (i.e., departmental) consequences as well as global (i.e., institutional) ones. Faculty and department chairs in various disciplines may decide that some certain software would be useful in their curriculum and purchase it. But at the organizational level, decisions about course management systems are going to be made centrally, perhaps with faculty input, perhaps not. These decisions have large-scale consequences for faculty work.

Decisions about the instructional technology and distributed modes of learning are having substantial impacts on the composition, responsibilities, and working conditions of faculty members. These impacts raise job design issues as well as pedagogical design issues.

The discourse governing these decisions has moved far from their center in academic and pedagogical concerns, to concerns focused on costs and revenues and the practice of managerialism in the community college workplace. Faculty will have to work collectively and individually to regain control of the discourse and reassert their professional authority. Faculty control of the curriculum means not just working with the knowledge base of a discipline but controlling its production and presentation.

NEW DIRECTIONS FOR COMMUNITY COLLEGES • DOI: 10.1002/cc

- How can faculty participate proactively and provide leadership in the use of technology in learning environments and instructional processes?

At the level of systems of authority, Mintzberg (1983) describes how power in and around organizations can accrue to internal and/or external coalitions of interested parties. Is such an internal coalition possible in community colleges, among faculty, administrators, support staff, and students who want to see information technology used effectively but within a framework of a learning-based environment rather than as a cost-cutting tool? This is a question for the faculty members of each community college to ask themselves and to address together through unions and other organizational channels.

At the cultural level, there are models that can be used as starting points. One of the most important goals is to create environments that encourage variety and are not circumscribed by standardization. Bernbom (1997) distinguishes architectural and ecological approaches to information management. The architectural approach implies building from the top down and selects technologies and information practices according to a rational design. An ecological approach allows for random variation, is built from the bottom up, and selects technologies and information practices according to their utility, or fitness. Which approach does an institution take in establishing institution-wide information strategies? Or how are the best of these two approaches brought together in a single strategy? Bernbom notes that the ecological approach best describes the academic world.

Faculty, and administrators on the academic side, including the president, can participate proactively and provide leadership in the use of technology in learning environments and instructional processes. Kezar and Lester (2009) describe a program that institutions can follow to encourage grassroots faculty leadership across the organization, including technology. One has to examine who makes the decisions about the use of technology in instruction, at the institutional scale, the program and department scale, the course scale, the individual faculty member scale, and the student scale. Here are some suggestions, first in the realm of general principles and then with regard to technology itself.

Recommendations for Faculty Involvement in Using Technology

- Take responsibility for the overall educational program, especially quality.
- Understand the larger economic and social forces shaping the discourse about teaching and learning, and promote faculty and student values and perspectives in response.

- Recognize and act on other related issues within institutions that impact curriculum, such as the use and treatment of part-time faculty members and the need for strong participation mechanisms for faculty members overall.
- Work with administrators and support staff to find common ground on the role of technology in the institution.
- Work at the department, discipline, and institutional level to put these principles into practice at every opportunity.
- Address the underlying problem of disinvestment in higher education by advocating publicly.
- Be, and insist on being, involved in evaluations of technological systems and processes. Focus on their effectiveness in learning. Evaluate claims of cost effectiveness. Insist that management be involved. Create ongoing evaluation systems, not just one-time assessments.
- Use or create collective bargaining and governance system opportunities to participate in decisions about the use of instructional technology and its impact on workload and working conditions, professional development, and intellectual property.
- Consider Smith and Rhoades's (2006) typology of models (craft, collegial, and assembly line) to understand and guide the structuring of technology-based courses. Work to recognize and prevent the unbundling of faculty work.
- Consider open-source course management environments to encourage customization and to avoid becoming dependent on commercial systems.

This chapter has addressed the critical role of faculty in leading the integration of computer technologies into instructional programs of community colleges. Although large elements of the technical environment are externally driven, *how* they get used in the learning environment—in teaching and learning processes—is within institutional control. Creation of organizational systems and cultures that encourage faculty participation and expertise ensure that learning variation and technology exploration continue in an era during which standardization and cost/benefit pressures impact institutional choices.

References

Amey, M., and VanDerLinden, K. "The Use of Technology: Institutional Issues." *NEA Almanac of Higher Education*, 2003, 85–95.

Armstrong, S., Simer, L., and Spaniol, L. "Models of Technology Management at the Community College: the Role of the Chief Information Officer." In T. Treat (ed.), *Technology Management*. New Directions for Community Colleges, no. 154. San Francisco: Jossey-Bass, 2011.

Barber, B. "The Technology Think Tank: Dilemmas of Innovation." *Community College Moment*, 2010, X, 34–41.

Bernbom, G. "Institution-wide Information Strategies." *Cause/Effect*, 1997, *20*(1), 8–11.
Birnbaum, R. *How Colleges Work: The Cybernetics of Academic Organization and Leadership*. San Francisco: Jossey-Bass, 1988.
de los Santos, Jr., A. G., and Story, N. O. "Maricopa's Ocotillo: Connectivity for Curriculum, Technology, and Pedagogy." In G. E. de los Santos, A. de los Santos, Jr., and M. Milliron (eds.), *Access in the Information Age: Community College Bridging the Digital Divide*, 53–60. Mission Viejo, Calif: League for Innovation in the Community College, 2001.
Diaz, V., and Cheslock, J. "Faculty Use of Instructional Technology and Distributed Learning." In J. S. Levin, S. Kater, and R. L. Wagoner (eds.), *Community College Faculty: At Work in the New Economy*, pp. 63–79. New York: Palgrave Macmillan, 2006.
Dickson, R. "The Changing Role of Community College Faculty: Implications in the Literature. *Community College Review*, 1999, *26*(4), 23–36.
Dolce, P. C., and Morales-Vasquez, R. "Teaching the Importance of Place in the World of Virtual Reality." *Thought & Action*, 2003, Summer, 39–48.
Hanson, C. "Curriculum, Technology, and Higher Education." *Thought & Action*, 2008, Fall, 70–79.
Garza Mitchell, R. L. "Online Education and Organizational Change." *Community College Review*, 2009, *37*(1), 81–101.
Garza Mitchell, R. L. "Approaching Common Ground: Defining Quality in Online Education." In R. L. Garza Mitchell (ed.), *Online Education*. New Directions for Community Colleges, no. 150. San Francisco: Jossey-Bass, 2010.
Gonick, L. "The Year Ahead in Higher Ed Technology." *Inside Higher Ed*, January 6, 2009. Retrieved July 24, 2010, from http://www.insidehighered.com/views/2009/01/06/gonick.
Green, K. C. "LMS 3.0." *Inside Higher Ed*, November 4, 2009. Retrieved July 24, 2010, from http://www.insidehighered.com/views/2009/11/04/green.
Kezar, A., and J. Lester. "Supporting Faculty Grassroots Leadership." *Research in Higher Education*, 2009, *50*, 715–740.
Kezar, A. J. "Exploring New Avenues for Leading Community Colleges: The Paradox of Participatory Models." *Community College Review*, 1998, *25*(4), 75–87.
Kezar, A. J. "Understanding and Facilitating Organizational Change in the 21st Century," *ASHE-ERIC Higher Education Report*, *28*(4). San Francisco: Jossey-Bass, 2001.
Levin, J. S. "The Buffered and the Buffeted Institution: Globalization and the Community College." In B. K. Townsend and S. B. Twombly (eds.), *Community Colleges: Policy in the Future Context*, pp. 77–100. Westport, Conn.: Ablex Publishing, 2001.
Levin, J. S., Kater, S., and Wagoner., R. L. *Community College Faculty: At Work in the New Economy*. New York: Palgrave Macmillan, 2006.
Maitland, C., Rhoades, G., and Smith, M. F. "Unions and Senates: Governance and Distance Education." *NEA Almanac of Higher Education*, 2009, pp. 75–84.
March, J. G., and Olsen, J. P. *Democratic Governance*. New York: Free Press, 1995.
Mintzberg, H. *Power in and Around Organizations*. Englewood Cliffs, N.J.: Prentice Hall, 1983.
Rhoades, G., and Maitland, C. "Bargaining Workload and Workforce on the High Tech Campus." *NEA Almanac of Higher Education*, 2004, 75–81.
Scott, W. R. *Organizations* (3rd ed.). Englewood Cliffs, N.J.: Prentice Hall, 1992.
Shpancer, N. "What Makes Classroom Learning a Worthwhile Experience?" *Thought & Action*, 2004, Winter, 23–35.
Smith, D. R., and Ayers, D. F. "Culturally Responsive Pedagogy and Online Learning: Implications for the Globalized Community College." *Community College Journal of Research & Practice*, 2006, *30*(5/6), 401–415.

Smith, V .C., and Rhoades. G. "Community College Faculty and Web-based Classes."
    Thought & Action, 2006, Fall, 97–110.
Villanti, C. "Educational Issues." In American Federation of Teachers Higher Education
    Department, *Technology Review: Key Trends, Bargaining Strategies and Educational
    Issues*, pp. D-1–D-6. Washington D. C.: American Federation of Teachers. 2003.

*BOB BARBER was a community college computer instructor and faculty leader
for twenty years, most extensively at Lane Community College in Eugene,
Oregon, from which he retired in 2007. He earned his Ph.D. in higher education
leadership from the University of Oregon, while teaching, in 2002.*

8

Community colleges provide a wide range of educational services to very diverse groups of students. For that reason, the variety and flexibility of services provided can be critical. In addition, quickly changing needs result in quickly changing system requirements. In this chapter, community college CIOs speak to their roles, focusing on the critical issues they face today and the approaches their institutions are taking to ensure preparation for a rapidly changing technological future.

Models of Technology Management at the Community College: The Role of the Chief Information Officer

Scott Armstrong, Lauren Simer, Lee Spaniol

Budget Development

As the landscape of higher education continues to change, community college chief information officers (CIOs) face challenges in uncharted territory. Few CIOs arrived in the position following the same career path; most have varied backgrounds and experiences on which to draw. As colleagues, generally speaking, CIOs openly share lessons learned with one another and offer their expertise on projects and strategies or survival tips for maneuvering through political and social cultures. With enrollments rising, budgets tightening, technology demands increasing, and state funding dropping below the market value of funding from the early 1980s, CIOs have become

New Directions for Community Colleges, no. 154, Summer 2011 © 2011 Wiley Periodicals, Inc.
Published online in Wiley Online Library (wileyonlinelibrary.com) • DOI: 10.1002/cc.449

quasi-experts on finances in order to understand funding sources and pursue ways to maintain existing technology as well as to fund new technology. However, it should be noted that most CIOs develop strong working relationships with chief financial officers (CFOs), respecting and valuing their expertise in providing guidance throughout the budget process. The CFO is an indispensable ally, seeking funding sources and explaining their intricacies so the CIO can focus on improving technology.

Before the CIO can begin the process of developing a budget or a technology plan, the institution must have a clearly defined institutional strategic plan that includes a goal of continuous improvement. This process of defining what the institutional priorities are and implementing a program of self-assessment will then allow the CIO to align the technology goals, resources, and strategies with the institutional budget. If the institution has a clear strategic plan, the CIO will have a clear direction to guide the information technology (IT) strategic plan, develop a budget, direct decisions related to systems and services, and create a functional IT governance model. The critical need for an institutional strategic plan cannot be emphasized strongly enough.

As part of an effective technology plan, an institution should consider how and when technology hardware can or should be replaced. Most colleges have been fortunate enough to receive grants to assist with technology purchases; however, these grants usually only fund new equipment and do not consider infrastructure costs such as cabling or the equipment that supports the client systems purchased with grant monies. Projectors, computers, laptops, personal digital assistants, and netbooks are all added to the inventory and need to be replenished as they age, as does the equipment to support them. One way to view the budget process is simply to inventory all the equipment, cabling plants, servers, switches, routers, phones, computers, projectors, document cameras, monitors, and the like and plan a mass replacement of all equipment at once. Doing this would ensure that everything is up to date and compatible and would reduce repairs on equipment for a period of about three years, the length of most equipment warranties.

Another option is to establish a replacement cycle of a percentage of systems, equipment, cabling plants, and the like per year. For example, if it were determined that computers should be replaced every four years and servers every six years, a plan could be developed determining how many pieces of equipment needed to be replaced each year for a full cycle. Once the total annual expense was determined, funding sources could be identified. Realistically, it may be that the equipment replacement cycle is extended or in some instances shortened to accommodate available funding and to meet the needs and priorities of the college.

A third option might be simply to identify a number of systems annually to be replaced and, based on the CIO's recommendation, the board of trustees approves a specific number of replacements. Leasing equipment may be an attractive alternative, depending on the circumstances of the individual institution. The lease agreement usually allows for a percentage of systems to be replaced annually, thus keeping the equipment continually updated.

There are a number of ways to fund equipment replacement cycles, including operating funds, bond issuance, technology fees, and grants. Once again, the CFO is best able to explain these options in detail; this chapter is meant only to provide a broad overview. As a general rule, most grant opportunities have strict restrictions and often fund technology for new or innovative programs. It is difficult to find grants to support replacement of existing technology, as replacement is considered part of the cost of operating the institution and should be built into the strategic planning process. Operating funds historically have been allocated to support plant operations, but as state funding cuts and state-allocated funds for technology have gone by the wayside, it is increasingly more difficult for community colleges to fund technology upgrades from operations.

Bonding can be a reasonable way to fund technology upgrades with a couple of caveats. It cannot be stated too often that a strategic plan plays a crucial role in ensuring that taxpayer money is being spent judiciously. A carefully mapped technology plan based on an institutional plan with self-assessment and continuous improvement built in will ensure oversight and guide expenditures during the bonding cycle. The institution must show it is financially sound and present a clear financial road map before a bond will be approved. If the board of trustees decides to pursue bond funding for special projects, the CFO will develop such a road map. It will be incumbent upon the CIO to ensure that the funds appropriated for any technology projects or upgrades are spent as detailed in the bond.

One final source of funding is a technology fee. The technology fee is an extra fee charged to students per credit hour of enrollment. This amount can fluctuate from semester to semester, but it is usually not part of operations; it is a separate revenue line item. It can be: allowed to accumulate from one semester to the next, over a period of years, to plan for a large-ticket project; used for operations, such as software maintenance renewals, to free up the operational budget for other items; or set aside to fund the hardware upgrade plan. The downside is adding fees to students' ever-increasing cost of tuition, books, and fees.

IT Governance and Provisioning of Systems

In the role of developing budgets, it is essential for the CIO to develop an alliance with the CFO. In discussing the role of the CIO provisioning systems and services, collaboration with others throughout the institution is integral to the success of the institution, and the strategic plan is integral to the prioritization and provisioning of systems. Indeed, division chairs, directors, program coordinators, and individual faculty members all have unique technology requirements from an academic perspective. Vice presidents, directors of service areas, deans, and individual departmental staff members all have unique technology requirements from a service and support perspective. How then does a CIO effectively service these often competing priorities? Several models have proven successful and, generally speaking, CIOs employ them all to some extent, forming a hybrid model that is unique to each institution. Each model has some form of IT governance in play, with openness and transparency built into the governance. It is imperative that the CIO present all sides to all involved in the governance system employed.

One model of IT governance would be through the use of a technology committee. This collaborative committee could be comprised of technology-savvy employees from all areas of the institution represented. The CIO then has a responsibility to this committee to demonstrate the needs of respective projects and to work with the committee to prioritize and fund those projects that best align with the strategic plan. With this governance structure, members of the technology committee must have the entire organization in mind, setting aside individual and departmental needs. They also must be accountable to others within their respective areas when projects are prioritized.

A second model of IT governance that can be successful is via the leadership team of the institution. The leadership team generally is made up of the president, vice presidents, and department heads, potentially including division chairs and supervisory staff as well. The same basic premise applies to this model as applies to the technology committee with collaboration being a central theme. The CIO has the responsibility of demonstrating needs of respective projects and working to fund those projects that best align with the strategic plan. This model has some inherent positives, one of which is the fact that, generally speaking, the leadership team has the entire organization in mind when making decisions. Likewise, the leadership team generally has a better understanding of financing and budgeting. This model certainly lends itself to ensuring that the budget is in place for not only this year's projects but for those of subsequent years. In fact, during the budget cycle, this model allows those projects that align with the strategic plan to rise to the top on their own.

Neither model of IT governance can solve all of the issues of competing priorities in these times of tight budgets and scarce staff resources. There are inevitably times when the CIO will have to tell someone a project will have to wait due to resource constraints. In those instances, what tools can be employed to smooth that process? One way is to identify how all requested projects align with the strategic plan. Projects can be prioritized based on their alignment with the institutional strategic plan. This method still does not solve the problem when twenty projects align with the strategic plan, and there is staff and funding available to complete only ten of them. A second pass through those twenty projects could be completed, identifying wants versus needs. It is only through the collaborative efforts of all involved with each project that wants versus needs can be established. It is possible that all twenty projects could be completed, if scaled back to complete only the parts of the project that satisfy "needs," leaving the "wants" on the table. "Wants" would go through the budget cycle to be funded in future years.

An alternative is to use some form of return on investment (ROI) calculation for all requested projects. This method is difficult to implement because individuals requesting project funding do not have a solid understanding of the financial tools and information required to develop the ROI. Keeping in mind that the first pass is always alignment to the strategic plan, projects that pass the alignment test next have an ROI developed. The first project implemented would be the one with the highest ROI. The second project would demonstrate the next highest ROI, and so on until the funding and scarce resources are consumed.

Introducing New Technologies

Another significant challenge in the process of provisioning systems and services is how to introduce new systems, make them functional, and provide training to those who manage and use them. One way to implement new systems successfully is through the tried-and-true process of piloting. This collaboration with a subset of users in which each has the responsibility to and accountability for the areas they represent during the implementation ensures broader success of a large-scale project implementation. These pilot users typically go on to become the proponents of the system and provide the groundwork for developing whatever training would be required for the larger rollout. The often-neglected issue using the method of piloting is end user support when it comes time to expand the pilot. At some point in time, users will expect to be able to call the help desk and have someone knowledgeable about the product help them. Another method to implement new systems successfully is via full-blown project planning. This method requires the hard work of developing the project on paper—including all of those often-underestimated tasks such as training the help desk, training the end users, ensuring backup and recovery processes are in place, developing service-level agreements, user acceptance testing, and so on—on the front end of the project. One of the biggest benefits of this type of implementation, however, is that generally there are fewer bumps in the road to completion and fewer surprises during implementation.

Ever-Expanding Role of the CIO

The challenges of the ever-expanding role of the CIO encompass not only the selection and introduction of new systems and the development and delivery of end user training for those new systems but also the need for the IT department to keep pace with the new technologies while replacing obsolete ones efficiently. IT staff training can be a significant investment and should be considered part of the project budget for new or significant IT projects whenever possible. Although determining the costs of initial training may be relatively easy, estimating the costs of training to take into account staff turnover and continuity can be difficult. Experience and a thorough review of historical project costs can serve as guidelines when estimating such training costs.

With the challenges of keeping current with technology and innovation comes the need for innovative training solutions. Traditional classroom training environments already have been enhanced (or even replaced) by synchronous and asynchronous Web-based training, but some other training opportunities may not be as mainstream or obvious. Conferences may include dedicated training sessions, but user group conferences likely will be rich with shared end user experiences as well as reliable resources and tested and proven solutions. Vendor contracts can be negotiated to include train-the-trainer sessions during the knowledge transfer portion of a system implementation, sometimes at a steep discount, and well-established relationships with some vendors can result in both formal and informal training and shared expertise.

Once IT staff members are trained, their skill sets and resources still may not be enough for the next big project, and simply hiring more people may not be the answer. The initial and recurring costs of installing and maintaining a system or implementing a service can be mitigated by hiring expertise outside of the organization's IT department. By using consultants for initial installation, configuration, and knowledge transfer, an organization can pay for expertise as needed without committing to long-term employment contracts. Alternatively, arranging for hosted, cloud-based, or even outsourced systems and services can take advantage of the service organization's existing efficiencies and skill sets, eliminate the initial cost of hardware and installation, reduce or eliminate the costs associated with maintaining the system, and ultimately let an organization focus on system use rather than on system maintenance and support.

The decision to use cloud-based or hosted services, software-as-a-service (SaaS), or even contracted support, however, will be unique to each organization and will depend on the strategic goals, value of the services, mitigation of any risks, and ultimately the budget. As with any system, service, or project, the determination to use outside resources must align with the strategic plan and be within the budget.

NEW DIRECTIONS FOR COMMUNITY COLLEGES • DOI: 10.1002/cc

Although cloud computing currently is riding the wave of high-tech hype, eventually it will give way to some other new service or system that will be the answer to every organization's dream. Exposure to the "next new thing" is very important for the CIO and for the IT department, as the department will play a key role in introducing the new systems and services to the organization and in determining their functional and strategic value. Knowing how the "new thing" works is much less important, though, than knowing how it can or cannot fit into the organization's strategic plan. As previously discussed, an institutional effectiveness plan that includes continuous process improvement, self-assessment, and effective use of data to determine priorities and alignment with student learning outcomes is key to understanding what technology, new or existing, will best fit the organization's needs.

The collection and use of good metrics is important for any process and can help identify the amount of effort that must be expended in support of a system or service. Such information enables data-driven decision making, better supporting the determination of whether a given system requires more resources than it should and whether to replace it with a more efficient and cost-effective solution. Tracking time spent on system configuration, user training, and subsequent system issues will provide useful metrics in determining the amount of time and resources needed to support a given project and whether to shift priorities to other tasks or projects. Often a department will have anecdotal evidence to support a system requiring more attention than it should, but having numbers that can be equated to dollars and hours will be very useful when determining if such systems are, in fact, aligned with the organization's strategic plan. The systems that provide the most benefit and require the least support will be the most efficient systems in an organization. Absent good metrics, the CIO's task of finding and implementing the right improvements or replacements for inefficient systems can be particularly challenging. In all cases, each decision should support the organization's strategic plan, and that plan needs to have as its primary goal maintenance of the organization's competitiveness. Efficient systems in terms of support and costs will most certainly be an organization's competitive advantage.

The CIO also often is seen as the responsible agent for another set of difficult-to-manage challenges, namely end users' influences on the security and integrity of the organization's systems. As people become more comfortable with consumer technology in the home, they expect that same comfort and the associated personal flexibility in the workplace, and they expect to be able to use their personal devices at work. Smart phones with wireless networking capabilities, digital cameras, compact high-capacity portable digital storage devices, a plethora of Web-based user services, and easy access to every type of software on the Internet can enable a user environment that often is in conflict with the systems and practices designed to secure the organization's systems, making the job of securing systems and information a nightmare. Not only can users threaten the integrity of the systems and information, but they can present themselves to the rest of the world through freely available systems, sometimes appearing as a representative of the organization. Controlling the use of personal computing devices, limiting access to outside systems programs that pose a security risk, and educating the employees on the organization's policies and expectations will help control several of the CIO's user-influenced challenges.

The loss of physical systems now is overshadowed by the loss of data and personal information. Well-developed policies, procedures, and practices are required to ensure that end users understand the implications of their actions as they interact with the information-rich systems. With notebook computers and other mobile devices so prevalent in the workplace, the potential for the loss of the device is magnified by the loss of any sensitive information stored on those devices Policies, procedures, and practices should be designed to protect sensitive information in the case of the loss of a device, to limit the storage of sensitive information to appropriate systems only, and to encourage responsible use of systems that can access sensitive information are crucial.

Summary

We have discussed the role of the CIO in developing budgets, aligning those budgets with a strategic plan, and methods for devising a replacement cycle. We talked about the importance of IT governance; provisioning systems and technology services for those projects that are identified outside the typical boundaries of the IT area at the institution.

Next we would like to discuss briefly the role of the CIO in the area of innovation. CIOs, with their unique perspective on technology, have the responsibility and accountability to look forward to identify the next best thing that fits within the priorities of the strategic plan. Current examples of innovative technology include software as a service, cloud computing and thin client implementations. Regardless of specific example, the key role for a CIO is to stay abreast of new technologies while ensuring that what is implemented is solving a business problem, not buying into the hype and the latest buzz word.

Adding to the CIO's challenges associated with aligning projects with the strategic organization's goals and prioritizing project development within the available budget, the role of the CIO continues to change and expand under the influences of improved technology, innovative solutions, and resulting end user demands. Effective institutional strategic plans that include a continuous improvement assessment process, collaboration with colleagues, and maintaining a focus on student learning outcomes will ensure successful integration of technology within any institution.

SCOTT ARMSTRONG is director of information technology at Kishwaukee College, Malta, Illinois.

LAUREN SIMER is vice president for institutional effectiveness at Greenville Technical College, Greenville, SC.

LEE SPANIOL is director of information systems and services at Lake Land College, Mattoon, Illinois.

NEW DIRECTIONS FOR COMMUNITY COLLEGES • DOI: 10.1002/cc

9

In times of difficult funding, information technology managers must build new foundations, rationale statements, methods of operating, and measures of accountability to maintain a strong funding base to sustain information technology.

IT Funding's Race with Obsolescence, Innovation, Diffusion, and Planning

Jeff Bartkovich

In a time of economic uncertainty, discussing the funding of information technology (IT) for community colleges or higher education in general is difficult. For most community colleges, funding is dependent on public support, and agencies that disperse public funds are dealing with a delicate balance of taxes and services. The impact of dealing with public funding issues can change, and is changing, the way colleges approach their budgeting process. The rules and methods used to request external funds and the way those funds are allocated within the college have changed. Within these changes, institutions must build new foundations, new rationale statements, new methods of operating, and new measures of accountability to maintain information technology's funding base.

In 2010, as it has been since Educause began conducting its annual survey of IT issues, funding IT is at the top of the list (Ingerman and Yang, 2010). In recent years, funding IT has been the top critical issue for the strategic success of the campus, as assessed by chief information officers (CIOs). What seems to have changed over time, as noted in the 2010 commentary, is a clarification of how and why IT is important as a funding issue. The shift, in broad terms, has been from sufficient IT funding to *build* capacity to IT funding to *sustain* capacity to meet critical needs.

These two items, economic uncertainty in funding higher education and the importance of IT within colleges, are especially noteworthy in community colleges. Community colleges have a unique public mission,

NEW DIRECTIONS FOR COMMUNITY COLLEGES, no. 154, Summer 2011 © 2011 Wiley Periodicals, Inc.
Published online in Wiley Online Library (wileyonlinelibrary.com) • DOI: 10.1002/cc.450

typically are dependent on public funding to a greater extent than other sectors, have programs and services that are connected to workforce demands and changing student demographics, and have IT operations with few economies of scale. Consequently, funding IT in the community college must be driven by purpose, not by necessity, and as a strategic partner in the operations of the college, not as a utility.

IT Funding Sources in Community Colleges

The adage that no two community colleges are alike is especially true when budgeting is discussed. Community college budgets are a unique and challenging combination of student tuition (sometimes regulated), student fees (sometimes regulated), federal funding, state funding, local funding, and a host of other agencies that enter and leave at various times for various purposes. As various sources undergo modification due to changing fiscal situations, those in charge of IT funding may find it increasingly difficult to sustain operations at the annual budget level; that is, the annual allocation of general-purpose dollars from the college's maintenance and operating budget.

Few funds come to a college without restrictions. State and local funds are tied to mission tenets of access and workforce development. Federal funds are tied to special programs and financial aid. Student fees typically are reviewed and approved by local boards or state offices. Consequently, planning for IT funding needs to begin by targeting requests and requirements specific funding sources based on use. For example:

- State and local funds are good sources for ongoing services, operations, and personnel that support the general academic and business needs of the college.
- Student fees can be used to support the general technology infrastructure of the college or, if they can be earmarked, can be a significant ongoing source of technical funds for student support, such as e-mail or a technology help desk, original technology projects, such as netbooks for automotive students, or classroom technology.
- When tied to new construction, capital funds may be the only source for new infrastructure or major technology systems upgrades. Capital funds also can be targeted for annual capital renovations and improvement if the college defines technology infrastructure as a capital investment.
- Local bonds and tax levies, although not available to all community colleges, can be an important source of major technology dollars for upgrades to college-wide systems (cable and fiber networks, computer labs, classroom presentation technology), or for the implementation of new college-wide systems (Voice over Internet Protocol [VoIP], fire alarm network).

NEW DIRECTIONS FOR COMMUNITY COLLEGES • DOI: 10.1002/cc

- Leases and lease-to-purchase agreements are a purchasing process that has value for upgrading or installing a new technical system that spreads the cost at a manageable level over several years.
- Pay-for-services and charge-back are funding techniques that can serve a large community college with a significant demand for an ongoing service by a large number of users. Although primarily a management technique, pay-for-service can help to fund a high-cost project by distributing the cost to multiple users over time.

Three important concepts underlie the review of funding sources for IT:

1. Funding sources for community colleges typically are purposeful, outcome-specific, and intentional. IT funding is justified and sustained based on general purposes tied to the community college budget allocation process. However, in times of economic uncertainty and fiscal constraints, IT funding needs to identify clearly its projects and needs and tailor its requests to specific funding sources.
2. The concept of funding IT for the sake of having technology is no longer (if it ever was) true. Many new projects will need to have a clearly articulated purpose and clearly defined funding sources associated with the purpose. Local and state funding through annual appropriations will sustain operations, but new technology and new services will require new funding sources.
3. IT funding is no longer just an IT function or responsibility; it belongs to the college.

IT Funding Race in Community Colleges

General economic uncertainty and ongoing issues with IT funding in higher education are impacting the general availability and allocation of funds to community colleges and, subsequently, to IT. However, financial support for IT is not always just about money: how much and to whom, from what source for what purpose. Other internal issues within community colleges are changing the way funds are justified, allocated, and accounted for. These issues may bring more dollars into the IT budget or may divert technology dollars into non-IT budgets. Four issues that are being discussed and resolved on community college campuses are avoiding obsolescence, supporting innovation, addressing diffusion, and allying with planning.

Obsolescence. The rate of change in and from technology that community colleges must absorb and respond to is remarkable. Consider the college that is sued by students because the computer labs had old technology that hindered them from gaining employment. Consider the student who finds the home or the local coffee shop has more wireless capacity than the college. Consider the faculty member who wants to teach the most current Office Suite package, but the computer lab has old motherboards. Consider the administrator waiting for enrollment figures as the mainframe batch-loads data from the day before. From a technology perspective, community colleges have an image of being competitive with senior colleges, being on par with local industry, capable of training graduates with needed workforce skills, and being vibrant centers of technology exploration and application. IT budgets must be sufficient to support these community expectations. Obsolescence in any of the situations just mentioned can influence a community college's image.

The strain on IT budgets to avoid obsolescence is significant. Avoiding obsolescence goes beyond IT hardware and programs and must include annual software licenses, maintenance contracts, and highly competitive personnel costs. The rapid pace of replacement and need to use noninstructional calendar time to avoid impact on students is also an issue for IT funding. When implementing new technology to replace old technology, two budgets may overlap. Another issue is that even though the new technology may improve productivity, the additional costs of the new technology may not be reflected in the IT budget. IT funding, which is built to maintain existing levels of technology and services, needs flexible budgets to bridge these opportunities. Today's technology dollars purchase more computer power and more bandwidth than yesterday's dollars, but tomorrow's needs and technology consumption will push these dollars' value to obsolescence.

Innovation. If avoiding obsolescence is a necessity, is supporting innovation a luxury? The ability for IT budgets in times of limited resources to support research and development (R&D) or to experiment with new technology is likewise being constrained. Funding innovation is doubly difficult because, as mentioned, annual IT operating budgets are basic and intended to support ongoing operations, and because few external funding sources will fund innovation and experimentation. Funding innovation is not just an IT issue; it impacts many offices and individuals. However, innovations funded in a non-IT department may require new technology resources not funded in the IT budget. Additionally, annual department budgets may include funds to support efficiency measures, to automate manual processes, to purchase new applications in order to increase productivity. These efforts have IT funding implications without the IT funding attached.

For community colleges, innovation may be not a luxury but a necessity, on par with avoiding obsolescence. Beyond simple availability of dollars, funding IT innovation evokes the concept of return on investment (ROI). Can IT budgets be invested in principal funds today in expectation of principal and dividend funds tomorrow? Innovation implies risk, and putting scarce fiscal resources at risk in a time of economic uncertainty can be a dilemma. One perspective is that since IT will change and will adapt to new hardware and programs, the assessment and evaluation of new products will depend, unless some R&D is funded, on vendors or other users. Relying on such outside sources may or may not be acceptable, and adaptation of findings to local college needs might prove difficult. Funding innovation can facilitate testing of a product in the unique environment of a campus classroom or office. Since technology is user-driven, funding technology innovation also can build future user support. Finally, IT funding for innovation can be a diversion of basic operational dollars, but it also can be a catalyst for the generation of new operational dollars.

Diffusion. Experienced community college faculty or staff members who can remember back twenty years ago will understand the breadth and depth of change that has occurred with technology. Until quite recently, IT in the community college consisted of a monolithic mainframe service protected behind secured doors. IT funding was likewise monolithic and secured. As computers moved out of the data center, they brought with them new applications, new costs, new benefits, and new business operations. The mystery of computers moved from data automation to management information systems and data-driven decision making. The technology of computers moved from the central mainframe to distributed, always-on, just-for-me desktop units. These changes moved the funding decisions from IT departments into the open in two significant ways.

1. IT funding moved from a single department with a centralized budget to a distributed budget among multiple accounts in multiple departments.
2. College-wide and "system-level" decisions were moved to the executive boardroom, not because of the technological sophistication of the decision but because of the coordination needed among competing interests and the substantial costs.

Both changes allowed IT funding to meet the needs of the college and the changing features of technology. They also encouraged technology funding to be based on investment models that considered hardware costs and personnel savings as well as value added to the user. Both changes diffused the monolithic budget.

Today, the benefits of technology much more accessible delivered by campus networks (cable, fiber, wireless). Once the potential power of the mainframe, the systems, and external networks (i.e., Internet) are delivered, IT funding can be allocated to any department at any level to support program and equipment connectivity to the network. Various IT network applications can be significant, can be college-wide, and can be outside the authority and responsibility of the IT department and budget. In times of fiscal constraints and level budgets, the diffusion of existing IT funds *from* central projects needed to support systems infrastructure or ongoing programs *to* different departmental initiatives can be detrimental. Likewise, the diffusion of IT funds *from* low-profile, high-impact needs *to* high-profile, low-impact needs can be detrimental to the delivery of IT support to college-wide programs. To address this issue, a fully developed and communicated technology plan can set priorities for the allocation of IT funding based on value to the college, compatibility with network requirements, and functionality. Implied in this diffusion of technology funds and projects is the expectation that IT funds to maintain and advance the basic infrastructure that support the diffusion remain an executive priority.

Besides accessibility, a second principle of technology that relates to diffusion is integration. IT systems have grown in importance and complexity at community colleges for many reasons. One reason is their ability to integrate data from different sources, communications from different mediums, and applications from different sources all onto a common platform for output. These integration abilities are not without cost. As noted earlier, dollars spent for hardware and bandwidth increase value, but this does not follow for dollars spent on software. The costs for programming or purchasing an enterprise-wide application that builds functionality and integrates multiple applications are significant. The conflict for IT funding is that efforts to support access to technology by diffusing it, or to strengthen technology use through integration, may be in conflict with fiscal management efforts. IT serves best when it meets the diverse needs of many users. IT serves best with it integrates diverse applications onto common platforms. From a funding perspective, however, IT fiscal management performs best when it manages centrally the procurement and deployment of college-wide systems.

Planning. Responding to uncertain fiscal conditions within the context of its mission will challenge many community colleges. As community college budgets remain level, redistribution and conservation of funds will become a way of business. College-wide funds and their management will be viewed as an integrated process. In times of financial restraint and increasing service demands, efforts to secure stable and responsive IT funding will require diverse revenue sources and well-conceived plans. Maintaining quality of services while responding to growth and personalization of applications will require creative approaches to IT funding. These fiscal challenges also will require IT to approach fiscal management in innovative and responsible ways. Support from various funding sources and cooperation with various college departments will be important factors in the success of IT funding to support access, to provide integration, to avoid obsolescence, and to nurture innovation.

In many community colleges, IT funding is just one more item added to the list of budget agenda items that receive executive-level review. Enhanced scrutiny comes at a time when, due to the dependence of community colleges on dwindling public funds, competition for external distributions and internal allocations of funds is increasing. However, IT funding is brought to the budget table for two important reasons: its necessity and its costs. IT can be a critical solution in responding to administrative issues, such as processing student applications and records, storing and retrieving data, and communicating with students. IT's importance for information management and mainstream business practices, in turn, raises the importance of making decisions about technology and allocating funds for it. As the demands for IT become more complex, the technology of IT becomes more complex; as college dependence on technology increases, so does the importance of technology. IT hardware costs, IT software purchases and maintenance costs, IT programming costs, and IT project implementation costs are all significant and often require a multiyear commitment. A balance between a centralized budget and a diffused budget is required to secure the IT funding necessary to support all aspects of a college's operations and to ensure efficient and responsible use of funds.

Technology systems are costly to develop and manage. Consequently, increasing technology costs will present a significant financial challenge to a community college's budgeting process. Planning for technology must be a balance among providing access, building integration, and advancing innovation. This balance is not easy to achieve or sustain, but the relationship of technology to other aspects of the institution demands it. Technology expands access. Technology improves pedagogy. Technology supports operations. Securing funding for technology, therefore, is to supports all aspects of a community college's mission. Many community colleges are beginning to realize that IT funding is not just about ongoing operational expenses; it's about investing in the plans of the college.

Considering IT funding in the context of supporting the mission of the college has consequences. Will the solution promote excellence in teaching? Will the solution enrich the student experience? Will the solution expand enrollment? Will the solution address workforce needs? Will the solution build human capital? Will the solution respond to fiscal challenges? At times, IT may provide the right solution, but other solutions may prove more practical or beneficial when advancement of the college mission is the central question.

In tight fiscal times, the annual operating budget of community colleges may get first priority for the allocation of funds. Planning funds and investment funds may be deferred to address the immediacy of the current year's budget. However, components of IT operations should not be left to annual discretionary accounts. Given the complexity, costs, and importance of IT, technology services and equipment should not rely on allocation methods that are uncertain or variable. Planning for and funding IT should be a continuous comprehensive process across several dimensions. Guided by the college's vision, IT funding needs to look at the full spectrum of college demands and needs and recognize that these demands and needs range over time and over purpose. Matching IT needs with college funding methods and sources of funds that vary in time and purpose is critical, as illustrated by the five examples below.

NEW DIRECTIONS FOR COMMUNITY COLLEGES • DOI: 10.1002/cc

- When public funding support is level, IT needs a funding source to supplement operational budgets to address increasing costs for major administrative systems that support users, add to productivity, and so on, such as student information systems, online commerce, document imaging. A general all-purpose technology fee assessed by the college to all students can be a significant and ongoing revenue source.
- When particular services and technology are student-driven or justified primarily by student demands, a specific student technology fee may be assessed by a student-centered nonprofit association or student government. These funds typically target a specific demand and typically are accounted for by the approving authority. These targeted enrollment-driven funds can be substantial, can be ongoing, and can serve the college's plan.
- Depreciation funds generally are used by community colleges to address the funding of high-cost, institution-wide projects and items that need cyclical replacement, such as carpets and furniture. These funds are drawn from a college-wide general fund, and the funds are allocated on a schedule. Certain IT items could be included in this funding category, such as classroom technology that is replaced on a six-year basis, or a scheduled projector bulb plan, or a centralized computer deployment plan that rotates computers on/off campus on a regular basis.
- Annual capital improvement funds, which recently at many campuses have become less reliable and more strained, may address IT funding for large-cost items where replacement is on an extended-years basis. The fiber network of a campus or the telecommunication core switches, both of which are high cost and need replacement every eight to ten years, could be justified in an annual capital improvement fund. Technology for this funding method is justified based on the argument that certain technology systems are part of the critical infrastructure systems of the college.
- When IT needs funds to begin new projects, to conduct R&D, or to respond to an executive request to launch a new initiative, a technology project fund or technology venture fund can provide needed support. Technology funds are for development and implementation, not for operations; they are meant to be one time, not ongoing. These funds also may be tied to the college's strategic or technology plan. Both such plans should have been through a college-wide process of development and have a college-wide project funding committee.

For many community colleges, institutional budget processes are tied to state or local accounting systems which dictate how funds are categorized, what funds can be used across fiscal years, what items can be classified as capital, and other specifics within these various accounting systems and definitions.

In conclusion, four key concepts have particular relevance for planning IT funding. First, IT funding, in the best-case environment, should proceed from four categories of funds: annual operating funds, infrastructure or capital replacement funds, annual project-specific or strategic funds, and research or venture funds. IT funding from new capital funds is also an option for major system upgrades or as a component of new facilities. To the extent possible, these four categories should be funded annually and protected from short-term public-funded variability. Their placement within the college operating budget as a budget account, as opposed to being treated as a discretionary item or add-on request, is likewise critical. These four categories will allow IT funds the needed flexibility to provide the systems and services required by the college. Second, IT funding beyond the current operating budget should be tied to the college's mission and strategic plan. If derived from the strategic plan, the IT budget should represent an operational item for the strategic plan. Third, IT funding plans should be comprehensive to reflect the complexity of the community college's academic and business operations and should be collaborative to reflect the integrative benefits of IT systems. Finally, IT funding should be held to the same standards of assessment and outcome evaluation requirements as the projects and programs it supports.

Reference

Ingerman, B. L. and Yang, C. "Top-Ten IT Issues, 2010." *EDUCAUSE Review*, 2010, 45(3), 46–60.

JEFF BARTKOVICH *is vice president for education technology services, Monroe Community College, Rochester, New York.*

10

Today's society is marked by massive political, social, and scientific transformations on a daily basis. However, these transformations are rarely discussed in the context of what it means to be an educated person. Our efforts to forecast, even for periods as little as five or ten years out, have been predicated on the assumption that the current rate of progress will continue into the future. A brief analysis of data—at all scales and scopes, in different time scales, and for a wide variety of technologies ranging from the electronic to the biological—illustrates that our notion of static rates of change is incorrect: Change, progress, and advancement are all happening at an accelerating rate. This chapter provides a presidential perspective on these trends to suggest that students of tomorrow must be educated in very different ways our institutions must adapt to be ready.

What is Next? Futuristic Thinking for Community Colleges

Thomas Ramage

The times in which we live are marked by massive transformations: politically, socially, and scientifically, and on what feels like a daily basis. Our efforts to plan and forecast, even for periods as little as five years distant, have been predicated on the assumption that the *current rate* of progress will continue into impending periods (Kurzweil, 2001). Author and inventor Ray Kurzweil calls this the "law of accelerating returns."

According to Kurzweil, if we were to study a wide variety of technologies ranging from the electronic to the biological, via a multitude of gradations and measures, we would find that our commonly held belief in a static rate of change is misguided. Change, progress, and advancement are occurring at an increasing rate (Kurzweil, 2005).

Yet for the volume and sheer impact of such transformations, it is a rare occasion that we discuss such startling change in the context of what it means to be an "educated person." With a few exceptions, our ideas about what it means to be an educated person are virtually the same as they were in

New Directions for Community Colleges, no. 154, Summer 2011 © 2011 Wiley Periodicals, Inc.
Published online in Wiley Online Library (wileyonlinelibrary.com) • DOI: 10.1002/cc.451

1892, when the first university preparatory curriculum was developed in the United States (Mitchell, 1981). This set of competencies remains largely intact today. One might agree in concept that the educated person should have an understanding of history and social issues, have an appreciation of literature and poetry, be able to deal with matters of economics, understand scientific principles and the basics of mathematics, and, as a crowning achievement, be able to speak and write in more than one language.

Those descriptors were used to develop the high school curriculum in the United States in 1892. With the appointment of the Committee on Secondary School Studies (commonly called the Committee of Ten) under the chairmanship of Charles Eliot, president of Harvard University, these objectives were considered foundational for anyone who wanted to attend a university. Additionally, the committee recommended the same universal course of study for everyone, including those who had no intentions of attending college.

During the past 120 years, our investment in K–12 education in constant dollars per student has grown by a factor of ten.[4] We have experienced and absorbed a *hundredfold* increase in the number of students enrolling in postsecondary education. Why? For the past two centuries, according to Massachusetts Institute of Technology economist Frank Levy, automation has been eliminating jobs at the bottom of the skill ladder while creating new and better-paying jobs at the top, and it has caused the United States to increase investments in education exponentially at all levels (Levy and Murnec, 2005).

Globalization and automation have an effect on the job market as well. The assumption that these forces are "killing" the job market in the United States has been a common theme. Although there is some truth to this belief, shifts in employment trends in our current economy seem to happen faster and affect a great many more people.

Today, China is the largest global producer of toys, clothing, and consumer electronics. Automobiles, telecommunications, computers, biotechnology, and aerospace are next. China has 1.5 billion people whose factory wages start at 40 cents per hour. The minimum wage in the United States was set at 40 cents per hour on October 24, 1945 (Whittaker, 2003).

Today, there are 45,000 Taiwanese contract factories; there are 20,000 in Europe and 15,000 in the United States (Einhorn, 2005). Between 1995 and 2002, the world's twenty largest economies lost approximately 22 million industrial jobs. The United States lost about 2 million, mostly to China. In that same time frame, China lost 15 million, mostly to *machines* (Stokes, 2008). Competition comes in many different forms these days.

Economist Levy also tells us that there is a simple rule for deciding if a job is going to last in the United States or not. "*If you can describe the job precisely, it's gone.*"

For example, if you can write a rule for a job that says "If this happens, then do that," the job probably can be sourced to a computer or outsourced overseas. Levy goes on to say that this concept is disproportionately affecting what he calls the "middle-area jobs." Low-skill jobs that involve a lot of interpersonal contact are probably safe for the short term. High-skill jobs that require specialized knowledge, creativity, and/or proximity to others are likely safe for now also. But those jobs that are in between, that operate under a set of rules or decision points, are at significant risk.

Today, public expectations and our high school curriculum remain remarkably static, with the exceptions of a call for accountability, national standardized assessments, and second-class status for any student who chooses a path other than traditional baccalaureate preparation. What actually is the future for which we prepare our students? What impact does rapidly accelerating change have on what it means to be an educated person today or in five years?

Change, progress, and advancement appear to happen at an accelerating rate, and our educational systems are stressed proportionally. A couple of generations ago, we could learn from our parents most of the things we needed to survive and thrive. Education, defined broadly, consisted of the passing of knowledge from one generation to the next in a somewhat linear and orderly fashion. Today, there are too many new things to understand: nanotechnology, DNA, networks and computers, genetically modified organisms, global and interconnected financial systems, and quantum mechanics, to name just a very few. Examples help. Let us start with the most profound: human life expectancy.

Kurzweil's law of accelerating returns, when applied to human life expectancy, illustrates the fact that in the eighteenth century, technology, in general terms, added a few days each year to human longevity. During the nineteenth century, technology's impact on longevity grew to a couple of weeks each year. Today, we are adding almost half a year every year to life expectancy, due almost exclusively to the impact and availability of technology. Growth curves illustrating the number of human genomes mapped per year, the number of top-level Internet domains created every twelve months, and the decreases in size of mechanical devices (nanotechnology) have moved from a linear to an exponential scale.

Of course, this discussion is incomplete without reference to the fact that Moore's law, which predicts that the number of transistors that can be placed on an integrated circuit and the corresponding speed at which these chips can compute will double every eighteen to twenty-four months, seems to be alive and in force until at least 2015 (Stokes, 2008).

Human Genome Project

The first Human Genome Project centers were created in 1990. When work began, it was thought that it would take about one hundred years to get the first human genome sequenced, based on the computational power available to the consortium at that time (U.S. Department of Energy, 2010).

Fast forward to April 2003, some thirteen years later: The first sequence was completed at a cost of more than $500 million. Using the same technique, but with more advanced computers, a human genome could be decoded for a mere $10 million in 2006. Two years later, in February 2008, a company called Illumina did it in four weeks for $100,000 (Lauerman, 2008). Five weeks later, Applied Biosystems accomplished it in a couple of weeks for $60,000 (Davies, 2008). As of June 2009, Complete Genomics, which offers DNA analysis services to drug makers and other companies, began sequencing human genomes for $5,000 (Timmer, 2009). A $500 million process was reduced to $5,000 in six years due almost exclusively to advancements in computer processing power.

Consider the Trajectory of the Gigaflop

"FLOP" or "FLOPS" is an acronym meaning *floating point operations per second*, and its use is a measure of a computer's performance. A gigaflop represents 10^9, or about 1 billion floating point calculations per second.

It took humanity roughly 111 years (1900 to 2011) for our understanding of computing to evolve from the very first concept of a computer to that of an $84 gigaflop. In 1961, the extrapolated cost of 1 gigaflop of computing power was in neighborhood of $1.1 trillion. In 2007, a gigaflop could be had for $48; today, it costs about $1.80 (Afrit, Le Du, and Stevenson, 2011).

Assuming past performance is an indicator of future performance, it will take just seventeen years to develop a computer that has roughly the equivalent computing capacity of a human brain. This would allow 20 million billion calculations per second, give or take, for approximately $1,000 (Moravec, 1997). The next year, it will double again, as is the nature of exponential growth. Another twenty years after that, it is predicted that we will have a device with the capacity to compute at a rate equivalent to the entire human collective for about $1,000. That seems a little far-fetched, doesn't it?

Today, if one has $65 million, one can build a computer that is capable of sustained operation at 10 petaflops (10^{15}), or 1,000 trillion calculations per second. The University of Illinois at Urbana-Champaign, which is approximately five miles from the Parkland College campus, will put such a device online in 2011 (University of Illinois, 2010). Given past performance, this $65 million device should cost in the neighborhood of $1,000 in the span of about fourteen years, and this path assumes no amazing scientific advances or economic events, positive or negative. In fourteen years, $65 million halved fourteen times comes to just under $4,000. How does this exponential increase in computing power affect us and what does it mean? The implications are staggering. What in the world changes when this class of computing is possible? The short answer is *everything*.

Already, airplanes can take off and land on their own, the stock markets are monitored with predictive and recursive software systems, and doctors routinely use computer-aided diagnostics to care for their patients. What is the impact of all of this technology on our jobs, our lives, and our colleges?

First of all, there is a downside. The increasing complexity of our lives, without equal gains in our ability to manage, synthesize, and understand these impacts, is a major and growing concern. We human beings are not keeping pace well enough to avoid causing disasters due to human error. We need not look further than the oil spill in the Gulf of Mexico for an example.

For all of our advancements, we have yet to develop a method of harnessing the technology to advance the field of education. We employ roughly the same model that we did in 1892. I am reminded of the phrase "Were Rip Van Winkle to wake up today after sleeping for 130 years, probably the only thing he would recognize would be the typical school classroom" (Dryden, 2000).

Of course, this statement is not true. We are indeed in the middle of our own revolution, but it has far more to do with *access* to higher education made possible by technology and its advancement. Numerous studies exist that attempt to prove or disprove the impact of technology on the learner (Ramage, 2002). Perhaps the more significant question has to do with the number of people who are able to come to the well versus how deeply they drink. The classical tenet of access to higher education is fundamental and foundational in the community college (Vaughn, 1999).

Our mission of access is illustrated in technological terms on our campuses every day. Our students expect robust bandwidth to power their netbooks, iPhones and iPads, and laptops. They expect wireless signals (both Internet and cellular) to reach into every nook and corner of the college. They expect far more than a simple syllabus with the e-mail address of the professor.

At Parkland College, significant investment in faculty development, course redesign, and the required support systems began fifteen years ago. The administration, at the time, wisely invested resources in the creation of one of the first student and course management portals and engaged faculty in the selection and management of hardware and software. Today, the vast majority of class sections offered at Parkland College rely on learning management software, blurring the lines between traditional on-campus courses and those labeled as online or hybrid sections. Additionally, our faculty and staff have grown accustomed to electronic class rosters with student pictures and e-mail addresses, automatic population of the learning management system, online grading, and the ability to generate a multitude of reports on the fly.

Our students insist on networked access to their class schedules, financial aid portfolios, degree audit systems, and "live chat" with student services professionals, even at 1 A.M. *Especially* at 1 A.M. We attract students from all over the country as well as concurrently enrolled students at the

University of Illinois at Urbana-Champaign. Access and convenience in conjunction with quality and transferability are imperatives.

Institutionally, the proportion of capital dollars expended each year to purchase new computers and to refresh network infrastructure and servers appears to be accelerating as well. Today, we speak in terms of terabyte storage when it seems like just last semester it was merely gigabytes. Yet at the very same time, employers in the community college districts that we serve lament the very real deficits in our graduates' ability to communicate effectively, work in teams, and think critically. It seems as if we, in community colleges especially, are squeezed between the dichotomy of understanding this rapid change with respect to curriculum, equipment, and labs and watching our students stumble over the very basic work ethic skills instilled by our parents a generation before—so much so that we have developed a stand-alone course designed to address what were once "basic training" skills taught at home and modeled by family.

If we are able to connect these dots—accelerating returns, exponential growth in speed and capacity of computing, globalization, and technology—with a relatively static curriculum, should it surprise us that our most enduring mission in the community college is to provide pathways to work and to a decent living, our transfer mission included? It boils down to the fact that no matter how well intentioned our academic programs and rhetoric, a college education must provide the skills needed to get a job.

Today, I am sure of one thing: Change is constant, and its rate is accelerating exponentially.

We need not be futurists to conclude that the whole endeavor of higher education has been forever changed by these forces, perhaps none more significant than technology in the form of networked information systems. From the student's perspective, all if it—communications, entertainment, and learning—can and should be accomplished on a smart phone. Just as our systems have evolved in the past in pursuit of greater access for students, their insatiable appetite for quick and easy access to information must drive our system designs now.

References

Afrti, M., Le Du, Y., and Stevenson, A. "High-Performance Computing on Gamer PCs, Part 1: Hardware." *Ars Technica*, March 30, 2011. Retrieved April 15, 2011, from http://arstechnica.com/science/news/2011/03/high-performance-computing-on-gamer-pcs-part-1-hardware.ars.

Davies, K. "Applied Biosystems and the $60,000 Human Genome." Bio-IT World.com, March 13, 2008. Retrieved January 11, 2010, from http://www.bio-itworld.com/BioIT_Article.aspx?id=73334.

Dryden, G., "Nine Steps to Transform Education." October 2000. Retrieved April 15, 2011, from http://www.marthalakecov.org/~building/trans/international/dryden.htm.

Einhorn, B. "Why Taiwan Matters," *BusinessWeek*, May 16, 2005. Retrieved January 11, 2010, from http://www.businessweek.com/magazine/content/05_20/b3933011.htm.

Kurzweil, R. "Law of Accelerating Returns." 2001. Retrieved January 3, 2010, from http://www.kurzweilai.net/the-law-of-accelerating-returns.

Kurzweil, Ray. *The Singularity Is Near.* New York: Viking, 2005.

Lauerman, J. "Illumina Says It Sequenced Human Genome in Record Time, Cost." Bloomberg.com, February 9, 2008. Retrieved January 10, 2010, from http://www.bloomberg.com/apps/news?pid=newsarchive&sid=aAgJB2R0Wcqs.

Levy, F., and Murnac, R. "How Computerized Work and Globalization Shape Human Skill Demands." In M. Suarez-Orozco (ed.), Learning in the Global Era. 158-Berkeley: University of California Press, 2005.

Mitchell, R. *The Graves of Academe.* Boston: Little, Brown, 1981.

Moravec, H. "When Will Computer Hardware Match the Human Brain?" *Journal of Evolution and Technology*, 1997, 1. Retrieved January 10, 2010, from http://www.transhumanist.com/volume1/moravec.htm.

Ramage, T. "The 'No Significant Difference' Phenomenon: A Literature Review." *E-Journal of Instructional Science and Technology*, 2002, 5(1). Retrieved May 8, 2004, from http://www.usq.edu.au/electpub/e-jist/docs/html2002/ramage.html.

Stokes, J. "Understanding Moore's Law." *Ars Technica*, 2008. Retrieved January 10, 2010, from http://arstechnica.com/hardware/news/2008/09/moore.ars.

Timmer, J. "Complete Genomics Produces a Cheap—Well, $5,000—Human Genome." November 5, 2009. Retrieved January 10, 2010, from http://arstechnica.com/science/news/2009/11/complete-genomics-produces-a-cheapwell-5000human-genome.ars.

United States Department of Energy. "Human Genome Project Information." 2010. Retrieved January 10, 2010, from http://www.ornl.gov/sci/techresources/Human_Genome/home.shtml.

University of Illinois. "About the Blue Waters Project." 2010. January 10, 2010, from http://www.ncsa.illinois.edu/BlueWaters/.

Vaughn, G. *The Community College Story.* Washington, D.C.: Community College Press, 1999.

Whittaker, W. G., "The Federal Minimum Wage and Average Hourly Earnings of Manufacturing Production Workers." 2003. Federal Publications. Paper 235. http://digitalcommons.ilr.cornell.edu/key_workplace/235.

THOMAS RAMAGE is president of Parkland College in Champaign, IL.

INDEX